Sturmstaffel 1

Reich Defence 1943-1944 The War Diary

Sturmstaffel 1

Reich Defence 1943-1944 The War Diary

Eric Mombeek with Robert Forsyth and Eddie J. Creek

Technical Illustrations
Arthur L. Bentley

Colour Artwork
Thomas A. Tullis and Dennis Davison

CLASSIC PUBLICATIONS

First published in 1999 by
Classic Publications
Friars Gate Farm
Mardens Hill
Crowborough
East Sussex TN6 1XH
England

ISBN 0 9526867 9 1

Cover design and book layout by Colin Woodman Graphic Design

Origination by Colourwise Limited, Burgess Hill, England

Printed in Italy by Officine Grafiche DeAgostini

Contents

Introduction

The story of *Sturmstaffel* 1 has never properly or completely been told in the English language. It may never be. The passing of time and lack of records serve to ensure that. This is not intended to be – nor should it be perceived as – a 'definitive account'. In the pages that follow, the reader will discover the result of fragments of information – compiled from documentary sources and from the memories of the few survivors still alive today – accumulated over the past fifteen or so years by the authors during their respective research into this small and short-lived unit.

Eric Mombeek has corresponded with- and interviewed veterans during the course of researching his published study of *Jagdgeschwader* 4. Robert Forsyth also interviewed and corresponded with survivors of *Sturmstaffel* 1 during the early 1990s. In this book, the authors' research is supplemented with additional historical data drawn from many published, non-published, official sources and enhanced still further by a selection of rare, informative and evocative photographs.

There has been much speculation, purported truths, glamourisation and unashamed myth written about *Sturmstaffel* 1 – about the unit's volunteers and its hazardous tactical doctrine. The reader will find none of that here, just the facts as the authors have discovered them – to date.

The kind assistance of the following individuals is gratefully acknowledged:

Former members of *Sturmstaffel* 1 or their families (F): Erwin Bacsila (F), Franz X. Berger, Oscar Boesch, Günter Ehrlich, Richard Franz, Rudolf Fendt, Hans-Günter von Kornatzki (F), Wolfgang Kosse (F), Erich Lambertus (F), Gerhard Marburg (F), Rudolf Metz (F), Siegfried Müller, Heinz von Neuenstein (F), Helmut Nonnenprediger, Werner Peinemann (F), Fritz Reinsperger (F), Heinz Steffen (F), Otto Weissenberger (F), Othmar Zehart (F).

Other former members of the *Jagdwaffe*: Hans Berger, Herbert Eh, Horst Geyer, Wilhelm Moritz, Gerhard Sarodnick, Karl-Fritz Schloßstein.

Fellow researchers and aviation historians:
Nick Beale, Winfried Bock, Eddie J. Creek, Robert Foose, Roger Freeman, James H. Kitchens, Hans Lächler, Martin Pegg, Peter Petrick, Jean-Louis Roba, Barry Smith, J.Richard Smith, Werner Stocker, Jean-Pierre van Mol, Dave Wadman, Pierre Watteuw

E.M., R.F. & E.J.C.

1. RAISON D'ÊTRE

The Allied strategic bomber offensive waged against Germany between 1941-1945 has often – and justifiably so – been credited with bringing about the Third Reich's inability to continue the war. For nearly three years, almost day by day, night by night, the Allied air forces systematically pulverised Germany's industrial cities and production centres, bombed its oil refineries, paralysed its transport system, terrorised and killed its civilians and eventually smashed its armies as they defended their ever-shrinking territory.

As the offensive ground on, the *Luftwaffe*, charged with defending the skies over the Reich against such seemingly overwhelming and insurmountable odds, found it difficult to cope. This was a war of attrition; a bitter battle to defend the homeland which tested and stretched both material and human resources to their limits. Over the past thirty years, historians have recorded from varying perspectives and in considerable detail, the way in which the *Luftwaffe* fighter force conducted the *Reichsverteidigung* – the Defence of the Reich. German aviation technology triumphed and failed; the reputations of the finest fighter pilots of the *Jagdwaffe* – the so-called *Experten* – became legendary when the fruits of victory were being enjoyed, but were denigrated when the Nazi leadership sought scapegoats for the daily suffering inflicted on the people of Germany. The analysis has been endless.

> "I spent a few hours there, in the dark and dust, listening to the bombs falling above our heads. When we got out, the town was nothing but fire and ruins, a place like Hell. The following night, and the night after, the bombs fell again. I made up my mind. I would volunteer for the *Sturmstaffel* then stationed at Salzwedel..."
>
> *Uffz. Oscar Boesch, Sturmstaffel 1*

Crew members of a B-17 Flying Fortress hitch a ride out to their aircraft on bomb and ammuniton trailers at an Eighth Air Force base somewhere in England in early 1943. The officer in the foreground is sitting on a 2,000 lb (907 kg) bomb.

One area in which the *Luftwaffe* excelled however, was in its continual endeavour to develop, assess, refine and amend its tactics for operations against the American daylight heavy bomber force which formed the core of the Allied offensive.

Commencing in the summer of 1942, the USAAF sent its four-engined B-17 Flying Fortress and B-24 Liberator heavy bombers against targets in occupied France and, from January 1943, to targets in Germany. The early missions were, in truth, little more than small, shallow penetration raids mounted against harbour installations, shipping, railway yards and airfields, designed to allow RAF fighter escort to the target and back and though there was still a long way to go before longer range and larger missions could be planned with confidence, valuable lessons were already being learned through operational experience.

Equally, *Luftwaffe* tacticians and commanders quickly realised that it was no mean feat to bring down just one of the accursed and heavily armed "heavies" or *Viermots*.[1] A single B-17F, for example, carried up to twelve 0.50-in (12.7 mm) Browning machine-guns positioned to give maximum all round protection from fighter attack. Breaking through the escort in a Bf 109 or Fw 190 fighter to get close enough to the bombers to ensure success was a difficult and draining task. German pilots usually resorted to diving through the escort fighters, firing a burst with their machine guns at the nearest bomber before seeking refuge in cloud, followed by a quick return to base. As the range of the raids increased and the fighter escort reduced, so the *Luftwaffe* invariably attacked from the rear of the formation, but such a method resulted in heavy losses incurred from the bombers' intense rearward defensive fire and had an adverse effect on German morale. Often, the *Jagdflieger* were reluctant to press home an attack to close range, opening fire only at extreme and thus ineffective distances of around 1,000 m (1,000 yds).

In a revealing report prepared for the British Air Ministry in September 1942, an American liaison officer wrote:

"Gunners are given sectors to search so that all fields of view are covered. At least three guns may be brought bear on any point 400 yds from a B-17F. Mutual firepower from ships in formation greatly increases the number of guns that may fire at enemy aircraft attacking the formation."

"Enemy fighter attacks from all angles have been experienced. They started with stern attacks, went to quarter, beam, below, bow and on the last two missions, head-on attacks. The success of all these attacks has been about the same. The B-17s that have been shot down have been from the usual causes of straggling and gunners getting killed. Damage to airplanes returning has been slight, and there have only been two airplanes at any one time out of commission due to enemy gunfire. Gunners have caused many fighters to decide not to attack by firing a burst just as the fighter begins the turn-in to attack. This has been done on some occasions when the fighter was a thousand yards away or more."

In the right hands however, an Fw 190 A-4, armed with four 20 mm cannon and two 7.9 mm machine-guns could prove lethal. A three second burst from an attack by such a machine loosed off some 130 rounds from each set of guns. It was generally recognised that twenty 20 mm rounds were required to shoot down an American

A gunner on board a B-17 simulates taking aim with his 0.50-inch calibre M2 Browning machine gun which is located at the aircraft's waist hatch position.

The Fw 190 A-4, a robust, well-armed fighter used by the Luftwaffe against the early USAAF heavy bomber raids over North West Europe in 1942. Here an aircraft of 7./JG 2 is rearmed following a sortie over the Western Front. The armourers have removed the 200-round storage boxes for the wing-mounted MG 151s via the wheelwells.

Inset *Hptm. Egon Mayer, Gruppenkommandeur of III./JG 2, seen here relaxing with other pilots on the Western Front in the summer of 1942. Already a successful fighter ace who once downed 16 Allied aircraft in 21 days, Mayer was the key proponent behind the Luftwaffe's adoption of the frontal attack against American heavy bombers in 1942.*

Above *Mayer believed that a frontal pass, as opposed to the customary rearward attack against heavy bombers, offered the best chance to inflict damage on the vulnerable cockpit area. Even more importantly, the frontal arc of defensive fire was the weakest.*

heavy bomber, unless a shell managed to hit a sensitive area of the aircraft such as the wing-mounted fuel tanks. Analysis of gun-camera films led German tacticians and armament experts to believe that the average fighter pilot scored hits on a bomber with only some two per cent of the total number of rounds fired. Thus to obtain the necessary twenty rounds for a "kill", 1,000 rounds of 20 mm ammunition would need to be expended over a 23 second firing pass in an Fw 190 A-4, a dangerously long period for a rear-mounted attack. For the *Luftwaffe*, this meant one thing; the odds of success were against them.

But there was hope. On 9 October 1942, the US Eighth Air Force launched its strongest attack since commencement of operations, when a force of 108 bombers was despatched to bomb a steel plant and locomotive and wagon factory at Lille in France, plus a pair of fighter airfields. The Fw 190s of III./JG 26 scrambled out of Wevelgem and, led by the *Gruppenkommandeur, Hptm.* Josef Priller, climbed to intercept the American formation, which was now down to 69 machines due to forced returns. As the bombers turned left south of Lille, the Focke-Wulfs closed in from the rear in pairs. This time, the Germans launched sustained and persistent attacks. Priller saw his victim, a B-24, crash north of Lille. Elsewhere, German pilots saw how the engines of B-17s burst into flames under fire from their guns, forcing the bomber crews to bail out. In total the pilots of III./JG 26 accounted for four bombers shot down for the loss of one German pilot from 7. *Staffel.*

This was the high point of USAAF heavy-bomber effort in 1942 and it would not be until April the following year that a raid was launched which exceeded the strength of forces sent to Lille.

On 23 November 1942, a force of 36 unescorted B-17s and B-24s from the US VIII Bomber Command hit the U-boat base of St. Nazaire in France. As the B-17s made their bomb run, Fw 190s from *Hptm.* Egon Mayer's III./JG 2 swept in to meet them. The attack provided Mayer with the perfect opportunity to test a new tactic which had been the subject of considerable discussion among local fighter commanders for several weeks. Forming up into *Ketten* of three aircraft, the Fw 190s went into the attack from dead-ahead and at great speed, before firing a no-deflection burst and breaking away in a climb or half-roll beneath the bombers. Mayer believed that a frontal pass, as opposed to the customary rearward attack, offered the best chance to inflict damage on the bombers' vulnerable cockpit area. Even more importantly, the frontal arc of defensive fire was the weakest.

Four bombers went down following the attack, for the loss of only one Fw 190 A-4 piloted by *Uffz.* Theodor Angele, Mayer's wingman, who crashed into the sea. Effectively, from that moment, many considered that the B-17 was obsolete as a self-defending bomber.

Encouraged by this success, *Generalmajor* Adolf Galland, the *General der Jagdflieger* and a keen proponent of tactical innovation, issued a circular to all *Luftwaffe* fighter units in which he wrote:

"Close observation of the enemy defence during this and subsequent attacks brought the following facts to light:

"On the approach there was no defensive fire. In the get away after a sharp pull up to left or right, no defensive fire at first, then suddenly there was heavy defensive fire which first passed behind the German fighters but which however heavily hit the fighter as the bomber's range and altitude advantage increased.

"After this, several attacks were flown on Fortresses from front low and on the last attack, hits were seen in the fuselage and wing roots. In turning under the Fortress, a light ball of fire was observed under the fuselage and thereupon the Fortress spun in twisting and turning and exploded after receiving more hits from the rear.

"*Object Lessons*
a. The attack from the rear against a four-engined bomber formation promises little success and almost always brings losses. If an attack from the rear must be carried through, it should be done from above or below and the fuel tanks and engines should be the aiming points.
b. The attack from the side can be effective, but it requires thorough training and good gunnery.
c. The attack from the front, front high, or front low, all with low speed was the most effective of all. Flying ability, good aiming and closing up to the shortest possible range are the prerequisites for success.
d. The exit can succeed only in a sharp diving turn in the direction of the bomber formation or single bomber. The most important factor is the angle of curve in which the fighter leaves the bomber formation.
e. Basically, the strongest weapon is the massed and repeated attack by an entire fighter formation. In such cases, the defensive fire can be weakened and the bomber formation broken up."

The air war over occupied Europe and the Reich intensified throughout the first half of 1943. At the start of the year, the *Luftwaffe* had 635 fighters available in the west. Throughout the spring and summer, the Eighth Air Force conducted unescorted bomber missions against targets in northern Germany, whilst those mounted against targets in the occupied territories enjoyed the benefits of fighter protection. By July, P-47 Thunderbolts appeared for the first time fitted with auxiliary fuel tanks which greatly

Generalmajor Adolf Galland, the General der Jagdflieger, recognised the benefits of the frontal attack against heavy bombers as well as the crucial requirement of "meeting mass with mass". "...The strongest weapon is the massed and repeated attack by an entire fighter formation," Galland wrote in 1943. "... The defensive fire can be weakened and the bomber formation broken up."

A B-17 – FDR's Potato Peeler Kids – from the 1st Bombardment Wing leaves the French coast having bombed U-boat pens at Brest on 27 February 1943.

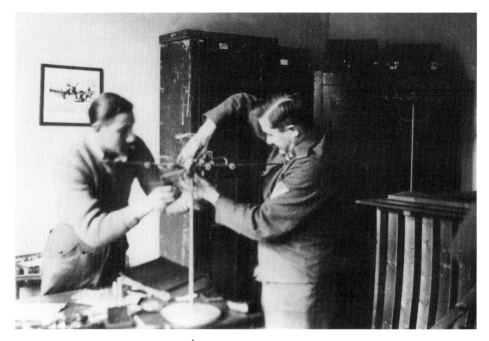

Staff personnel of 3./JG 1 assemble a model of a B-17 which will be used to instruct pilots on interception tactics. Note the cones of wire attached the model which serve to indicate the spread of defensive fire.

extended their range. On the 28th, the first occasion that they were used, the *Luftwaffe* waited until the escort had to turn back before launching their attack on the then vulnerable bombers heading for Kassel-Batteshausen and Magdeburg. As the German fighters hacked their way into the American formation, 15 bombers went down, 11 credited to JG 11 alone. Just three days later, over Kiel and Hamburg, another 19 bombers were lost.

German attack tactics at this time seemed to sway between attacks from the rear and from head-on. Those pilots electing to mount rearward attacks found that the most vulnerable spot on a four-engine bomber was the wing area between the fuselage and the in-board engines. The number three engine on a B-17 Flying Fortress was considered particularly important because it powered the hydraulic system.

In executing the head-on attack, which many units preferred, the cockpit and – once again – the number three engine became the most important targets. However, in August 1943, the OKL ordered that all attacks mounted against heavy bombers must be made from the rear, rather than by a frontal pass chiefly because, in their view, a large percentage of the young, inexperienced pilots now equipping the *Jagdgeschwader*

A model similar to that shown above is closely examined by pilots of JG 2 during the summer of 1943.

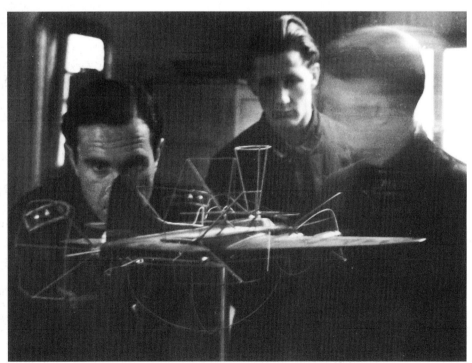

operating in the defence of the Reich and over the west, encountered considerable difficulty in undertaking the latter type of attack. The frontal pass involved a high combined closing speed which, in turn, demanded great skill in gunnery, range estimation and flying control. The slightest evasive action on the part of the bombers made this type of attack even more difficult. In contrast, evasive action taken against attacks from the rear, was thought ineffective.

On 17 August 1943, the US VIII Bomber Command launched its notorious and well-documented attack against the ball-bearing industry located around Schweinfurt. At 06.45, the first B-17s took-off from England for a mission which, in terms of size, surpassed anything that had gone before. The attack was carried out by two large formations. The first, comprising 146 B-17s from seven Bomb Groups belonging to the 4th Bomb Wing, would attack the Messerschmitt works at Regensburg-Prüfening and continue across southern Europe to land at bases in North Africa. The second formation, consisting of 230 aircraft from nine Bomb Groups of the 1st Bomb Wing had, as its objective, the ball bearing works at Schweinfurt. However, the unsettled weather over the south-east of England hampered take-off. Just when it was thought that the missions would have to be scrubbed, the order to proceed was given. Precious time had been lost and the raids had lost their synchronisation. It took more than an hour for the first wave bombers to join up and assemble into combat formation. The fighter escort joined them over the North Sea at cruising speed to maximise fuel economy. Shortly after 09:30, the complete formation crossed the Dutch coast south of the Scheldt estuary. At the same time, the order for take-off reached III./JG 1. The unit's 32 serviceable Bf 109 G-6s left Leeuwarden led by *Hptm.* Robert Olejnik and headed for Deelen airfield where they were to await further orders.

The neighbouring unit, *Jagdgeschwader* 26, established contact with the Allied armada over Antwerp. From this moment on, German fighters harried the bombers along their entire route over Europe. III./JG 1 took-off again and intercepted just as the escorting fighters, at the limit of their range, turned back over the Belgian-German border.

Hptm. Olejnik recalled the interception: "At a height of 7,500 m (24,600 ft), about 50 to 60 km (30-37 mls) away, I sighted three formations of bombers. I changed course towards them. At this time we were over the Aachen region. The enemy was flying on a south-easterly course. After a chase of 35 minutes, I made contact over Saarbrücken. By this time my *Gruppe* had already been in violent combat for a quarter of an hour, the sound of which had reverberated in my earphones."

"I gained height to weigh up the position. They were Fortresses, with their very impressive defensive armament. These aircraft were better left alone! Nevertheless, I

Hptm. Robert Olejnik (centre), Gruppenkommandeur of III./JG 1 relaxes with officers of his staff in 1943, Oberzahlmeister Hans Selbach (to the left) and Lt. Hans Halbey (Technical Officer).

A B-17 from the 4th Bombardment Wing pulls away from its bomb run over the Messerschmitt plant at Regensburg on 17 August 1943. Below, smoke drifts into the sky from the burning target.

attacked a bomber to the left of the formation from behind and slightly below. After my third attack, black smoke escaped from its right engine. Little by little, the enemy aircraft became detached from its group, but managed to correct itself 100 m (328 ft) behind, losing 80 m (262 ft) of height in the process – a very uncomfortable position for it; it could no longer count on the protection of its colleagues. It released its bombs, which was the prudent thing to do."

"During my fourth attack, the aircraft went out of control. Engulfed in flames, it made three large turns to the left. Seven crewmen bailed out. At 4,000 m (13,120 ft), the turns became tighter. The right wing broke off, followed by the left wing. The fuselage continued to dive and hit the ground in a wood near Darmstadt. Three men were probably still in the aircraft. It was high time for me to land. Towards 13:45 hours, I landed at Mannheim-Sandhofen, where my aircraft could be refuelled and rearmed. I found several of my pilots there, who had also chosen the base as a landing place. We were soon ready for further combat. In spite of that, we were ordered to take off late and we were not able to attack the *Amis* on their return flight. We had four wounded but claimed 12 victories ..."[2]

Other units took up the pursuit and the *Luftwaffe* attacked the bombers as far as Regensburg. Nevertheless 126 bombers were able to unload their deadly cargo on the factories. However, their ordeal was not over; heading for Africa, they had to get through German fighter units based in southern Europe. Exhausted, after a flight of 11 hours, the surviving crews finally touched down at Bone, Telerma and Berteaux. They had left 24 of their crews in Europe.

At 11:20, the 230 four-engined bombers of the second wave took off. They would also suffer heavy losses. One hour later, elements of I., II. and III./JG 1 and JG 11 intercepted a group of 100 B-17s. The massacre began; eleven B-17s were claimed by JG 1 and a dozen more by JG 11.

In total, 60 B-17s were shot down and 168 damaged. The Allies lost three P-47s and three Spitfires. But even the destruction inflicted upon the factories did not

B-17s of the Eighth Air Force's 94th Bomb Group leave the Focke-Wulf plant at Marienburg burning on the afternoon of 9 October 1943, following a mission which, for the first time, used 100 lb jellied gasoline incendiary bombs. The Marienburg facility was responsible for nearly 50 per cent of Fw 190 output at the time. The B-17s, flying at 11,000-13,000 ft, dropped 60 per cent of their bombs within 1,000 ft of their intended point of impact, while 83 per cent fell within 2,000 ft. General Ira Eaker described the results as "... a classic example of precision bombing."

By October 1943, Reichsmarschall Hermann Göring issued explicit orders that the prime task of German day fighters in the West was to intercept four-engine bombers. Göring is seen here during an inspection of fighter units at Achmer, late 1943. Behind him can be seen from centre left, Oblt. Werner Thierfelder (with Ritterkreuz and leather coat), Hptm. Horst Geyer, commander of Erprobungskommando 25, the Luftwaffe's anti-bomber weapons testing and evaluation unit, Major Hajo Herrmann, Kommandeur, 30. Jagddivision and Oberst Hannes Trautloft, the Inspector of Day Fighters.

compensate the loss of more than 600 Allied airmen – especially so when the truth was that German production was interrupted for only a few weeks. This time, the German fighter force was able to celebrate a cautious victory despite the fact that the losses for all participating *Geschwader* amounted to 17 killed and 14 wounded.

On 4 October, 155 B-17s with strong P-47 escort were assigned as their targets, the industrial regions of Frankfurt and Wiesbaden, as well as the city of Frankfurt itself. Towards 11:00, II./JG 1 intercepted and attacked a group of about 100 B-17s at an altitude of 8,000 m (26,246 ft) over the Eifel/Wiesbaden area. The first attack was from behind and at an angle and was mounted without success. Four Fw 190s were damaged by the defensive fire. While the *Gruppe* was reorganising itself for a second pass, it was joined by several pilots from I. *Gruppe*. During the attack four more Fw 190s were hit, but eight B-17s were shot down.

Oblt. Rudolf Engleder, the *Staffelkaptän* of 1./JG 1 recalled that day: "A tough encounter unfolded at an altitude of 9,000-10,000 m (29,520-32,800 ft). Once again, the imposing American fighter escort engaged us in a cloudless sky. The bombardment no doubt hit the Hanau industries hard, because those responsible for its defence and the *Gauleiter* of Frankfurt visited Göring and protested strongly about his fighters: *"How is it possible that American bombers can fly over the city in almost parade ground fashion? And further, German fighters were seen at altitude, not attacking!"* Göring went into one of his mad rages in which he knew the answer, and he despatched to all the fighter units responsible, the following orders, firstly, there are no meteorological conditions which will prevent fighters from taking off and engaging in combat, secondly, every fighter pilot who lands in a machine not showing any sign of combat, or without having recorded a victory will be prosecuted by a court-martial, thirdly in a case where a pilot uses up his ammunition, or if his weapons are unusable, he should ram the enemy bomber."

These directives, particularly the latter two, illustrate the desperate measures to which Göring was prepared to go to save humiliation in the face of Hitler, raise the ailing reputation of the *Luftwaffe's* fighter force and to preserve his still intact popularity with the German people.

The disturbing fact was that by the autumn of 1943, Göring had begun to isolate

Oberstleutnant Hermann Graf (left), Kommodore of JG 11 and the Kommandeur of I./JG 11, Hptm. Rolf Hermichen discuss operations, January 1944. By this time, both pilots were amongst the Luftwaffe's leading fighter experte. Thirty four of Hermichen's 64 victories were four-engine bombers.

Major Anton Hackl, who led III./JG 11, JG 76 and II./JG 26 during the latter half of the war, was accredited with the destruction of 34 four-engine bombers making him one of the Luftwaffe's leading "specialists" in this form of air combat.

himself from the reality of Germany's and, in particular, the *Luftwaffe's* worsening predicament. Throughout that year, he became increasingly dependent on drugs, and more and more absorbed in expanding his collection of art treasures and jewellery.

Cracks and strains in the relationship between the *Reichsmarschall* and his fighter commanders began to appear as early as the spring of 1943.

Göring demanded that his fighters stay airborne longer to deal with the bomber threat. When Galland endeavoured to point out the loss of manoeuvrability incurred by the outnumbered Bf 109s and Fw 190s based in France and the Low Countries as a result of carrying drop-tanks to increase flying time, Göring directed Galland to issue orders to the units that no pilot was to jettison his tank unless actually hit by enemy fire.

Later that year, as the Allied daylight raids intensified still further, Galland reasoned that it would be prudent to limit the number of machines and operations flown by the home defence *Geschwader* against individual enemy raids, so as to allow sufficient repair and re-grouping of aircraft which had landed on emergency fields. Only by carefully conserving strength and by efficient management of its most precious resources, namely its pilots, could the *Jagdwaffe* hope to cause any damage to the bombers. Unimpressed, Göring brushed this theory aside and demanded that all available units be thrown against every raid wherever and whenever possible. Nor, initially, were Galland's first reports of enemy fighter escort penetrating Reich airspace believed. According to Hitler's armaments minister, Albert Speer, shortly after the first American P-47 Thunderbolt escort fighter had been shot down over the German border in mid-1943, Göring had insinuated that the wreckage which his fighter commander had seen near Aachen had been the product of "...pure fantasy."

So it was, that as the *Jagdwaffe* began to suffer unacceptable levels of attrition during late 1943, Göring could only assume that the lack of any decisive victory over the Americans, a nation which, in any case, he considered capable only of manufacturing "fancy cars and refrigerators", was down to nothing but cowardice on the part of his fighter pilots. Had he not heard Galland talk of *Jägerschreck* – "Fighter Fear"?

In October 1943, Göring issued "explicit" orders to the Headquarters of I. *Jagdkorps* at Zeist in Holland to direct the efforts of those day fighter units under the *Korps'* command first and foremost against enemy four-engined bombers. The twin-engine *Zerstörergeschwader* – heavy fighters – were ordered to attack unescorted bombers and at the same time, instructions were issued that the equipping of certain units with 21 cm underwing air-to-air mortars was to be stepped up.

The war diary of I. *Jagdkorps* records that "... *the numerically inferior German daytime fighter units failed to prevent a single American large-scale raid during October 1943.*" Nevertheless, it also states that "... *the enemy suffered noticeable losses, especially in bombers...*"and, indeed, many of Galland's pilots were achieving unprecedented results and accumulating staggering scores against the hated *Viermots*. *Hauptmann* Rolf Hermichen of JG 11 was typical of the new ilk of "bomber-killers" who ended the war with 26 four-engined credits to his name. Pilots such as Hermann Graf, Walter Dahl, Anton Hackl and Kurt Bühligen were becoming household names. The highest scorer was *Oblt*. Herbert Rollwage whose 102 confirmed aerial victories, included 44 four-engined bombers.

And then there were the "innovators" – individuals and companies who came to Galland with their proposals for dealing with the bombers, some verging on the absurd others perhaps just workable; one was *Major* Hans-Günter von Kornatzki, a member of Galland's staff and a long-serving *Luftwaffe* officer married to one of Göring's secretaries, who, as a form of desperate response to the heavies, proposed the creation of a dedicated and specially equipped assault unit or *Sturmstaffel*. During the latter half of 1943 and at Göring's personal request, Kornatzki spent four weeks attached to *Erprobungskommando* 25 at Achmer. This unit was the *Luftwaffe's* specialist anti-bomber weapons and tactical evaluation unit. Equipped with his own Fw 58 *Weihe*, Kornatzki studied various possibilities and weapons intended for close-range work against bombers and he reported his findings with some diligence directly to the *Reichsmarschall*. During a meeting with Galland in the autumn of 1943, Kornatzki advocated adopting radical new tactics involving massed rear attacks against the bomber *Pulks* by tight formations of heavily armed and armoured Fw 190s.

Kornatzki had carefully studied reels of gun camera film, read combat reports describing attacks on *Viermots* and interviewed pilots. He reasoned that during a rearward attack against an American heavy bomber formation, one German fighter was potentially exposed to the defensive fire of more than forty 0.50-in (12.7 mm) machine-guns, resulting in only the slimmest chance of escaping damage during attack. Under such circumstances, it was even less likely that a lone fighter could bring down a bomber. However, if a complete *Gruppe* could position itself for an attack at close range, the bomber gunners would be forced to disperse their fire and thus weaken it, allowing individual fighters greater opportunity to close in, avoid damage and shoot a bomber down. The loss of speed and manoeuvrability incurred by the extra armament and armour carried by these *Sturm* aircraft would be countered by the presence of two regular fighter *Gruppen* which would keep any escort fighters at bay.

Kornatzki also suggested to Galland that, if necessary and as a last-ditch resort, in instances where pilots were close enough and if ammunition had been expended, a bomber could be rammed in order to bring it down.

He further proposed that a smaller unit – a *Staffel* rather than a *Gruppe* – first be established to train up volunteer pilots who would test and evaluate the new method under operational conditions.

It seems Galland needed little convincing. He immediately authorised the establishment of the first *Sturmstaffel* to be known as *Sturmstaffel* 1 and appointed Kornatzki its commander.

Major Walter Dahl, photographed at Finsterwalde in September 1944 whilst Kommodore of JG 300. On the 17th of that month, he brought down a B-17 by ramming. He is reputed to have accounted for more than 30 four-engine bombers.

Major Hans-Günter von Kornatzki studied reels of gun camera films and many combat reports. He reasoned that a mass attack made from the rear of a bomber formation would ensure less damage to German fighters and a offer greater chance of shooting a Viermot down.

---

1. *Viermot = lit. Vier-motor or Four engined bomber.*
2. *Despite Olejnik's statement, in fact, III./JG 1 is officially credited with only two victories for 17.8.1943, one of which was his. The question of overclaims – both Allied and Axis – is a reoccurring factor when studying the air war. In post-war correspondence, Olejnik emphasised how, following the chaos of a large air battle, it was difficult to ascertain which pilot should be officially credited with any given claim.*

2. WITHOUT REGARD TO LOSSES...

"The air war in the European Theater of Operations is becoming a slugging match between offense and defense. The side with the most stamina will win by a knockout..."

Extract from Target: Germany – The US Army Air Force's Official Story of the VIII Bomber Command's First Year over Europe (HMSO, London, 1944)

Hans-Günter von Kornatzki was born on 22 June, 1906 in Liegnitz, Silesia the son of *Generalmajor* Paul von Kornatzki and Gertrud von Briesen. He entered the *Reichswehr* on 9 May, 1928 and decided that he wanted to fly. Like hundreds of other young men of the time, Kornatzki's training took place amidst the clandestine conditions under which Germany was building its future air force. On 1 April 1934, he completed his fighter training at the *Fliegergruppe (S) Werneuchen* (later the *Jagdfliegerschule Werneuchen*) and three months later, transferred to the recently formed *Reklamestaffel Mitteldeutschland* at Döberitz. This unit eventually formed the nucleus of I./JG 132, the *Luftwaffe's* first fighter *Gruppe* under the command of *Major* Robert *Ritter* von Greim, to whom Kornatzki served as adjutant. A second *Gruppe*, II./JG 132 was formed in March 1935 at Jüterbog-Damm and Kornatzki transferred to it and was promoted to *Hauptmann*. He then joined I./JG 334 at Wiesbaden as *Gruppenadjutant* before transferring to I./JG 136 at Jever in 1938.

In September the following year, Kornatzki was appointed *Gruppenkommandeur* of II./JG 52 which saw brief service on the Channel Front during the Battle of Britain. The unit was based at Peuplingue, France in mid-August 1940, but returned to Jever after only a few days. It returned to France in late September.

In October 1940, Kornatzki returned to Werneuchen where he was posted to the staff of *Jagdfliegerschule* 1 and, from then on, he filled a number of staff assignments, finally serving on the *Stab General der Jagdflieger*.

Below *Hptm. von Kornatzki's Ar 68 E-1 after nosing over during taxying at Babenhausen-Hessen in 1937. At this time von Kornatzki was Gruppenadjutant of I./JG 334, his aircraft carrying a white bar and chevron marking. This marking was repeated on both sides of the fuselage.*

Right *On 3 May 1941, von Kornatzki married Ursula Grundtmann, a secretary to Reichsmarschall Göring and the daughter of a Generalmajor.*

Major Hans-Günter von Kornatzki.

On 3 May 1941, he married Ursula Grundtmann, a secretary to *Reichsmarschall* Göring and the daughter of a *Generalmajor*. The marriage was to be tragically short lived. Within two years, Ursula had been killed during an air raid on Berlin.

It has been said that the loss of his wife under such circumstances hardened Kornatzki's character and may have served to prompt him to devise radical ways in which to fight back against the Allied bombing offensive. Many of those who served under him however, remember that he cared for his men and that he never knowingly sent anyone cold-bloodedly to their death.

Lt. Richard Franz joined *Sturmstaffel* 1 in February 1944 having previously flown Bf 109s in Italy with 3./JG 77; he remembers: "I first met *Major* von Kornatzki in March 1944 when I arrived at Salzwedel, the home base of *Sturmstaffel* 1. There is a saying in German: *the first impression is always the right one* – and my first impression of him was as a very honourable officer, a gentleman. He was very calm and discreet, and yet tireless. Of course, there was a barrier; he was much older with the rank of *Major* whereas I was a *Leutnant*. But Kornatzki was a kind of father to us."

"We knew that he was close to Hermann (Göring), because he had been married to one of Hermann's secretaries and he drove an Auto-Union *Meisterklasse* car, a gift from the *Reichsmarschall*. But that was never a topic for conversation; we took that as a fact and that was all there was to it. Of course, we talked often about the *Sturm* concept and the tactics we were to use... about armament, armour-plating and so on."

"Kornatzki didn't fly often," remembers *Uffz.* Oscar Boesch, who joined the *Sturmstaffel* in late April 1944, "I never even saw him in an aeroplane! But he was like a father to the unit, he thought up tactics and worked very hard to ensure that we had everything we needed."

In early October 1943, Galland's staff scoured fighter bases and training schools across the Reich for suitable volunteer candidates for Kornatzki's fledgling unit. Though the initial response was meagre, eventually a cadre of 15 volunteer pilots was found, just enough to form a full strength *Staffel*.

These first volunteers were assembled and sent to Berlin where they met their new commanding officer. Kornatzki spoke to each candidate personally and explained the purpose of the unit and the inherent risks associated with the intended operations. Those pilots who showed signs either of a lack of conviction or of doubt or reluctance were "encouraged" to return to their former units.

One of the first pilots to be accepted was *Uffz.* Werner Peinemann, a former flying instructor with 1./*Jagdgruppe West* who left his previous unit on 19 October 1943 to join the *Sturmstaffel*. That same day also saw the arrival of *Gefr.* Gerhard Vivroux. Other volunteers included *Oblt.* Othmar Zehart, an Austrian who joined the *Staffel* in November; *Fhj.-Uffz.* Manfred Derp, who left JG 26 in November and arrived with the *Sturmstaffel* on 7 December; *Uffz.* Heinz von Neuenstein, previously with 7./*Jagdgruppe Ost* who also joined in December; *Uffz.* Erich Lambertus had only been with 2./JG 26 for a month before he volunteered for the *Sturmstaffel*, whilst *Uffz.* Otto Weissenberger arrived from 13.(Z)/JG 5, the *Geschwader* to which his

Below & centre
Uffz. Werner Peinemann and Gefr. Gerhard Vivroux were among the first pilots to join Sturmstaffel 1.

Left *Oblt. Othmar Zehart (second from left), an Austrian, joined Sturmstaffel 1 in November 1943. He is seen here with Major Erwin Bacsila (far left) and Lt. Hans-Georg Elser (third from left).*

Right *Uffz. Heinz von Neuenstein joined Sturmstaffel 1 in December 1943. He was killed in action at the end of the following month.*

Above *The brothers Weissenberger – from left, Otto, Theodor, Karl and Albert. Otto Weissenberger joined Sturmstaffel 1 at the end of 1943. His brother 'Theo' rose to the rank of Major and was awarded the Oakleaves to the Ritterkreuz in August 1943. He became Kommodore of the Me 262-equipped JG 7 and ended the war with 208 confirmed aerial victories.*

Ritterkreuzträger brother, Theodor, also belonged; 'Theo' had been awarded the Oakleaves to his *Ritterkreuz* in August in recognition of his 112 victories.

Other pilots transferred to the unit during its existence included *Gefr.* Heinz Steffen, *Lt.* Hans-Georg Elser, *Uffz.* Kurt Röhrich, *Ofw.* Gerhard Marburg, *Gefr.* Rudolf Pancherz, *Uffz.* Hermann Wahlfeld and *Flg.* Wolfgang Kosse. Kosse had seen service with JG 26 during the Battle of Britain, when he was appointed *Staffelkapitän* of 5./JG 26, a unit he commanded until May 1942 at which point he was transferred to a gunnery school. He was then posted to command 1./JG 5 and rose to the rank of *Hauptmann* before being stripped of this rank and demoted to *Flieger*, the lowest rank in the *Luftwaffe*, for having performed a forbidden flight in which he damaged an aircraft.

Further volunteers included *Uffz.* Walter Köst, *Fw* Josef Groten, *Uffz.* Willi Maximowitz, *Uffz.* Karl-Heinz Schmidt, *Uffz.* Helmut Keune, *Lt.* Friedrich Dammann, *Lt.* Wilhelm Münch, *Lt.* Gerhard Dost, *Uffz.* Karl Rhode, *Uffz.* Walter Kukuk, *Uffz.* Heinz Grosskreuz, *Lt.* Richard Franz, *Lt.* Werner Gerth, *Lt.* Siegfried Müller, *Uffz.* Günther Ehrlich, *Lt.* Rudolf Metz and *Uffz.* Oscar Boesch.

For good measure, *Generalleutnant* Galland ensured that Kornatzki's proposal went to Göring and on 8 November 1943, the *General der Jagdflieger* signalled his unit commanders:

"German fighters have been unable to obtain decisive successes in the defence against American four-engine formations. Even the introduction of new weaponry has not appreciably changed the situation. The main reason for this is the failure of formation leaders to lead up whole formations for attack at the closest possible range. Reichsmarschall Göring has therefore ordered the establishment of a Sturmstaffel whose task will be to break up Allied formations by means of an all-out attack with more heavily armed fighters in close formation and at the closest range. Such attacks that are undertaken are to be pressed home to the very heart of the Allied formation whatever happens and without regard to losses until the formation is annihilated."

Kornatzki also attracted support for his ideas at this time from *Major* Erwin Bacsila. Born in January 1910 in Budapest, Bacsila subsequently moved to Austria where he studied and later attended a military academy. Initially, he joined the artillery but then became a *Leutnant* in the *Flak* arm of the new Austrian air force in which he was one the first 50 officer pilots. He joined the German *Luftwaffe* following the *Anschluss* of 1938, rising to become *Gruppenadjutant* of II./ZG 1 during the Polish campaign. A respected officer, he was promoted to *Staffelkapitän* of 11.(N)/LG 2. On 15 September 1940, he took command of 7./JG 52, a position he held until September 1942, at which time he transferred as *Offz. z.b.V.* to the *Geschwaderstab* of JG 77 based in North Africa under *Major* Joachim Müncheberg. Bacsila flew as *Rottenflieger* to Müncheberg.

Right *Lt. Hans-Georg Elser flew with Sturmstaffel 1 throughout its operational existence. He was listed as missing whilst leading 3./JG 2 in December 1944.*

Far right *Gefr. Rudolf Pancherz left Sturmstaffel 1 in late January/early February to join 3./JG 11 with whom he was killed in action near Bremen on 3 March 1944.*

Subsequently, Bacsila left JG 77 and throughout 1943 took up command appointments in Russia and the West, including service as a *Jafü* in Brittany, eventually being posted to the *Sturmstaffel* in November of that year.

Fritz Reinsperger became *Staffeldienstoffizier*, a non-flying staff position.

Other pilots remained less convinced about Kornatzki's aims. *Major* Wilhelm Herget, a leading night-fighter ace and *Kommandeur* of I./NJG 4 recalled to his USAF interrogators after the war: "Kornatzki was the one who started out with the idea of ramming. But I personally pointed out to him: *"If you get to close enough grips to ram, you can be sure of shooting the enemy down too and you still have at least a fifty-fifty chance of getting down safely yourself."* It was out of this principle that the *Sturmgruppen* were born. Such ideas often took hold of the scatterbrains amongst us, who boosted their ideas very cleverly, dressed them up tremendously and carried them out ruthlessly."

On 17 November 1943, *Reichsmarschall* Göring visited *Sturmstaffel* 1 at Achmer accompanied by Galland. In their presence, the pilots were reminded of the strict code they were required to follow during their operations and were made to swear the following oath:

1. I volunteer for the Sturmstaffel of my own free will. I am aware of the basic objective of the Staffel.
   a. Without exception, the enemy will be approached in close formation.
   b. Losses during the approach will be immediately made up by closing up with the attack leader.
   c. The enemy will be shot down at the closest range. If that becomes impossible, ramming will be the only alternative.
   d. The Sturm pilot will remain with the damaged bomber until the aircraft impacts.
2. I voluntarily take up the obligation to carry out these tactics and will not land until the enemy has crashed. If these fundamentals are violated, I will face a court martial or will be removed from the unit.

As testimony to the seriousness with which this oath was sworn, the *Sturmstaffel* volunteers were also required to immediately draw up a last will and testament. At least one pilot, *Oblt.* Othmar Zehart, is known to have done so following this instruction.

However, *Uffz.* Oscar Boesch recalls: "We were not forced to sign the declaration, but, in a way, we had worked ourselves up mentally to succeed at any cost. We simply recognised the need to defend our homeland."

"The *Sturmstaffel* was unique. We were like a private club. We belonged to no one else except Göring. We had our own cook, our own ordnance. We lived like kings. Göring even sent down cases of Sekt when we had done well. Yet every day was a struggle to stay alive. We weren't after awards. The best award was to come back at the end of the day. We were outnumbered ten, sometimes twenty to one and we got tired, very tired, but we just kept going... We had to."

Above *Flg. Wolfgang Kosse. Kosse had originally held the rank of Hauptmann before being demoted to Flieger on account of making an unauthorised flight and damaging an aircraft. He joined the Sturmstaffel in the hope that he would regain his rank.*

Below *Major Erwin Bacsila, a respected Austrian officer who would help von Kornatzki in building up Sturmstaffel 1.*

Below left *Hptm. Fritz Reinsperger, Staffeldienstoffizier of Sturmstaffel 1.*

Below On 17 November 1943, the General der Jagdflieger, Generalleutnant Adolf Galland, visited Achmer where he inspected the men and equipment of Sturmstaffel 1 and Erprobungskommando 25, the anti-bomber weapons testing and evaluation unit. From left: Major Hans-Günter von Kornatzki, Galland, unknown officer of Erprobungskommando 25, Hptm. Horst Geyer, Kommandoführer of Erprobungskommando 25.

Above Genralleutnant Adolf Galland, a customary cigar clamped between his lips, is shown one of the latest items in Erprobungskommando 25's arsenal of anti-bomber weapons at Achmer. Peering over his shoulder are Major Hans-Günter von Kornatzki and Hptm. Horst Geyer.

Major von Kornatzki briefs his pilots ahead of their introduction to Generalleutnant Adolf Galland. Seen here – left to right – are: Major Erwin Bacsila, Major von Kornatzki, Gefr. Heinz Steffen, Uffz. Werner Peinemann, Gefr. Gerhard Vivroux, Uffz. Kurt Röhrich and Lt. Hans-Georg Elser.

Above *Major von Kornatzki presents Major Erwin Bacsila and Lt. Hans-Georg Elser to Generalleutnant Galland at Achmer, 17 November 1943. Hptm. Horst Geyer and other officers of Erprobungskommando 25 look on.*

Below *Deep in conversation, pilots of Sturmstaffel 1 walk with Adolf Galland across Achmer airfield. From left: Lt. Hans-Georg Elser, Major Hans-Günter von Kornatzki, Major Erwin Bacsila, Uffz. Werner Peinemann, Galland, Uffz. Kurt Röhrich, Gefr. Gerhard Vivroux and Gefr. Heinz Steffen.*

Left *Reichsmarschall Hermann Göring arrives for his tour of inspection at Achmer, 17 November 1943 and greets Major Hans-Günter von Kornatzki, commander of the newly-formed Sturmstaffel 1, with a fatherly hand on his shoulder. Standing in line next to von Kornatzki are Major Erwin Bacsila, Oblt. Othmar Zehart and Lt. Hans-Georg Elser.*

Below *Reichsmarschall Göring chats to Gefr. Rudolf Pancherz during his tour of inspection at Achmer. Also seen in this photograph are – from left – Major von Kornatzki, unknown, Uffz. Heinz von Neuenstein, (Göring), unknown, Uffz. Werner Peinemann, Gefr. Gerhard Vivroux, (Pancherz) and Gefr. Heinz Steffen.*

Right *Gerhard Vivroux and Heinz Steffen of Sturmstaffel 1 glance down the line of pilots as Hermann Göring walks past the Ritterkreuzträger, Hptm. Wolfgang Späte of Erprobungskommando 16 towards Hptm. Horst Geyer the commander of Erprobungskommando 25. Späte was at Achmer surveying airfield facilities for the possible operation of the Me 163 rocket fighter which was still under development at that time.*

Above One of the first Fw 190 A-6s to be delivered to Sturmstaffel 1 runs up its engine. Note the canopy has armoured quarter panels fitted and there is cockpit side armour fitted to the fuselage. Also of interest, is the dark fuselage band – not the black-white-black scheme usually applied to the unit's aircraft – and the dark cowling underside area. It is possible this aircraft had been allocated for transfer to JG 1, which provides an explanation for what is probably a red fuselage band.

Above "A private club": Major Erwin Bacsila together with some of the Sturmstaffel's first cadre of pilots at Achmer late October or early November 1943. Identifiable in this photograph are – far left, Uffz. Werner Peinemann, second from left, Uffz. Willi Maximowitz, fourth from left, Ofw. Gerhard Marburg, fifth from left, Bacsila and sixth from left, Gefr. Gerhard Vivroux. Behind the group, mechanics attend to one of the Staffel's Fw 190 A-6s. The armoured glass side panel mounted to the side of the canopy – better known a 'blinker' – is visible.

Below Freshly painted with their black-white-black fuselage identification bands, the Fw 190 A-6s of Sturmstaffel 1 are caught on camera for a newspaper propaganda photograph. In the background 'White 5' taxies past with the unit's lightning and gauntlet emblem just visible on its nose.

3. SHOOT DOWN THE FIRST TWO AND RAM THE THIRD...

January 1944

On 1 January 1944, *Sturmstaffel* 1 reported a total of 14 Focke-Wulf Fw 190 A-6s on strength, of which 11 were operational. Though the Fw 190 A-6 originated from a requirement for a heavy fighter for use on the Eastern Front, the *Sturmstaffel's* aircraft had been adapted for work against heavy bombers in the West and over the Reich. Powered by a BMW 801D-2 engine and developed from the Fw 190A-5/U10 (BP+LY, W.Nr. 861), the A-6 followed the A-5 onto the production line in the summer of 1943. Built under license by AGO, Arado and Fieseler, a fundamental design enhancement in the A-6 was the introduction of a lighter wing capable of accommodating increased armament in the form of four 20 mm MG 151/20 cannon located in the wing-roots and the outer panels, thus phasing out the old, slow-firing MG FF cannon.

Designed by Otto Helmutt von Lossnitzer and *Dr.* Doerge, joint directors of Waffenfabrik Mauser A.G., the electrically cocked and fired MG 151 had a rate of fire of 750 rounds per minute, discharging 86 kg (190 lb) of metal in flight at a muzzle velocity of 900 m (2,590 ft) per second. The weapon was recoil-operated and belt-fed, using a disintegrating metallic link belt. The MG 151 weighed 42.4 kg (93.5 lb).

Two fuselage-mounted 7.9 mm machine-guns were also retained and the aircraft

> **"One thing I can promise you; I shall not come back without two kills unless my engine is hit. I have made up my mind and I shall not fail..."**
>
> *Uffz. Heinz von Neuenstein, Sturmstaffel 1*

The Mauser MG 151/20 mm cannon.

Right *A newly completed Fw 190 A-6 in factory-fresh camouflage awaiting delivery to an operational unit.*

featured additional protective armour around the cockpit. The aircraft could be equipped with FuG 16ZE (as standard) and FuG 25 radio equipment.

Lt. Richard Franz thought highly of the aircraft: "The Fw 190 A was a very good aircraft in its *Sturmbock* version due to its armament and its additional armour plating. The radial engine also gave some protection. Due to its heaviness however, it showed a great disadvantage when engaging enemy fighters. In the normal configuration, the Fw 190 had some advantage in comparison with the Bf 109 up to 4,572 m (15,000 ft), whereas the Bf 109 was better at higher altitude."

When Sturmstaffel 1 transferred from Achmer to Dortmund, it joined the Fw 190s of I./JG 1 under Major Emil-Rudolf Schnoor which were already based there. The two units subsequently flew several missions together until late February 1944, when the Sturmstaffel moved to Salzwedel. Here a Fw 190 A-6 of I./JG 1 taxies past the hangars at Dortmund, early 1944.

"An excellent fighter aircraft," recalls *Uffz.* Oscar Boesch. "It was most reliable and robust. It was beautiful to fly according to my recollections and I was never outmanoeuvred. I had not flown the Fw 190 before I joined *Sturmstaffel* 1 and I only made four flights – one hour – in it before flying against B-17s. It was, of course, difficult to make comparisons in action since a) we were outnumbered by far, b) out positioned and c) over-worked and over-stressed. In general however, the P-51 Mustang was the most feared and dangerous opponent in every respect, both at high and low altitudes."

The aircraft used by *Sturmstaffel* 1 at this time lacked the 30 mm MK 108 cannon, perhaps the single most important item of armament needed in the battle against the bombers, but what was lost in armament was made up for in armour.

These initial machines constituted what was probably the first group of operational aircraft to be armour-adapted for close range anti-bomber work. Essentially, this adaptation involved the inclusion of 30 mm armoured glass panels – or *Panzerscheiben* – fitted around the standard glass cockpit side panels and a 50 mm plate of strengthened glass which would protect the pilot from fire from dead ahead. According to Focke-Wulf reports, some problems were experienced fitting the glass panels to the cockpit due to the angle of curvature of the cockpit's sliding hood, but these were eventually solved. According to a Messerschmitt report of April 1944, the *Sturmstaffel's* field modifications were undertaken in co-operation with Focke-Wulf but without sanction from the *General der Jagdflieger.* The installation of external 5 mm steel plates to the fuselage panelling around the cockpit area and the nose-cockpit join offered further protection from defensive fire. Additionally, the pilot's seat was fortified by 5 mm steel plates and a 12 mm head protection panel.

A later sub-variant, the Fw 190 A-8/R8 – the so-called *Sturmbock* – which saw service with IV.(*Sturm*)/JG 3, one of the *Gruppen* into which the *Sturmstaffel* would eventually be incorporated, also carried armour protection for its wing-mounted 30 mm MK 108 cannon.

In early January, *Sturmstaffel* 1 was transferred to Dortmund where it shared an airfield with the thirty or so Fw 190s of I./JG 1, under the command of *Major* Emil-Rudolf Schnoor. This *Gruppe* had gained considerable experience fighting the four-engine bombers of the US Eighth Air Force and some of the unit's pilots remember being approached to join the *Sturmstaffel* but it seems these attempts at recruitment met with little success. However, reservation on the part of other pilots was countered to some extent by the arrival from Italy of *Lt.* Werner Gerth, a tenacious pilot formerly with 7./JG 53.

Mechanics and engine technicians who were trained as specialists on the BMW 801 were also posted to the *Sturmstaffel* from the *Technische Vorschule* in München and had begun arriving throughout November and December.

Born in Upper Bavaria in 1923, Rudolf Fendt was a patriotic young man who had qualified as a Senior Mechanic in the *Luftwaffe*: "At the age of 14, I entered a military school in München where I was a boarder – though, in reality, it was like a barracks. One of the main courses there was engine mechanics, which meant that we had a lot of contact with the engine department at BMW which, in turn, provided us with a very good background for a technical career in the *Luftwaffe*. Because of this, I had early experience with the 14-cylinder BMW 801 radial engine that would later be used in the Fw 190 and by *Sturmstaffel* 1."

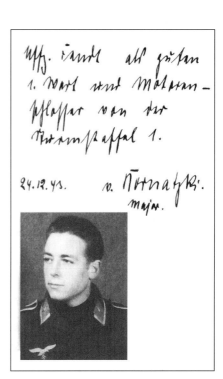

A photograph of Rudolf Fendt affixed to a piece of paper signed by Major von Kornatzki on Christmas Eve, December 1943. Fendt served as an engine specialist with Sturmstaffel 1.

Development of the Sturmflugzeug

When Hans-Günter von Kornatzki first proposed *Sturm* tactics there was no aircraft available to specifically carry out the task. It was, however, evident that the most readily available fighter aircraft at that time suitable for the job was the standard Fw 190 A-6.

Focke-Wulf documents dated 21 March 1945 give a complete breakdown of all the 'A' series variants and sub-types from the A-6 to the A-9, the last production model. Copies of these documents have been reproduced elsewhere in this book in their original form together with English translations.

Production of this heavy fighter commenced in June 1943 with manufacture undertaken by the Arado, Fieseler and Ago works. Two sub-types were also produced; firstly, the A-6/R1 with 2 x MG 151s under the wing, the conversion being undertaken by LZA at Küpper, near Sagan in Silesia, which was a subsidiary factory of the Arado company. Some 60 such aircraft were converted by 31 November 1943. The other sub-type, the A-6/R6 involved the retro-conversion of the '*Änderungs Anweisung Nr. 123*' (Conversion pack No. 123) for the fitting of the WGr 21 cm air-to-air mortar, which was also applied to remaining A-5 aircraft still in production. This work commenced at the beginning of November 1943 and by February 1944 was a standard installation for the whole A-6 series.

No mention is made of any special conversion work on the A-6 in an attempt to turn the aircraft into a *Sturmjäger*. Another point of note is that at least one manufacturer's

Possibly belonging to the Gruppenstab of I./JG 2, this aircraft is a standard Fw 190 A-6, W.Nr. 530941 and originally carried the radio call-sign SV+AA. The A-6 still carried the two MG 17 machine-guns as fuselage armament. No drop tanks were fitted as standard to the A-6 variant.

production line, probably Fieseler, constructed the A-6 without the inner undercarriage doors, but included the main undercarriage as fitted to the A-5 series which allowed for bomb racks and a 300 litre (66 gal.) drop tank to be fitted under the fuselage. A close study of some of the photographs in this book show that no inner undercarriage doors are visible but neither had the ETC 501 racks been fitted for the drop-tank installation. In addition, extra steel armour plating was added to the side of the fuselage around the cockpit area as well as a 50 mm (2 in.) armoured glass panel fitted to each side of the cockpit canopy. It is not known who carried out this modification but it could be that this was done in the field since the steel panels do not appear to be of a uniform size or fixed in the same place.

The A-6 production continued until November/ December 1943 when it was superseded by the A-7 variant. Series production began in November 1943 at the Fieseler and Ago works and in December at Focke-Wulf. The main change was that the MG 17 guns in the fuselage were replaced with two MG 131s. Other modifications are indicated on the Focke-Wulf documents.

Since the tactics of *Sturmstaffel* 1 were still to be properly evaluated in

The installation of twin MG 17 machine-guns in a Fw 190 A-3 with its BMW 801 engine removed.

combat at this point, it is likely that during the period of setting up the unit and in combat training, several problems were encountered. The MG 151 20 mm gun, for example, could not inflict as much damage as the new MK 108, 30 mm cannon, which had begun to appear at the end of 1943. Another comparison worthy of note, is that at this time of the war, the MG 151 was a weapon that required high precision engineering needing considerably more skilled labour and high quality metals. In comparison, the MK 108 was predominantly made from pressed and welded steel and required far less high precision manufacture and in consequence was also more expendable.

With the advent of the MK 108 another problem arose in that the standard A-6 and A-7 wing was unable to accommodate the gun inside the wing without some structural modifications. There were two sub-type variants of the A-7, the A-7/R2 and the A-7/R6. The A-7/R6 modification was the same as on the A-6/R6 but only 50% of the A-7 series production being so converted. It appears from the factory document, that the conversion work to the wing of the A-7/R2 was carried out by the

A Fieseler-built Fw 190 A-7, W.Nr. 642545, coded VQ+VC. The large '200' applied to the cowling may denote the 200th machine produced by Fieseler. Note that no drop tank equipment has been fitted.

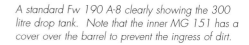

manufactured by Fieseler from February 1944 onwards which was eventually planned to become the series production sub-type A-8/R8. However no series production of the A-8/R8 was ever initiated because the full series production went straight to the next main production variant, the Fw 190 A-9/R8, which commenced series production at the GFW (Focke-Wulf) works in December 1944, followed by NDW (Nord Dornier Werk in Wismar) in February/March and Arado as of February 1945. The details regarding all the other main changes can be gleaned from the Focke-Wulf documents.

Further observation of the photographs in this book indicates that most of the *Sturmstaffel* 1 aircraft had the fuselage armament removed. The reason for this may have been that the increase in weight provided by the steel armour plating and extra glass panels considerably reduced the aircraft's performance and by removing these guns, which were not important in terms of close-range strike capability, the performance was much improved. Also none of the A-6 and A-7 aircraft were fitted with the BMW 801 GM power-boosted engine.

In conclusion and again looking at the photographic evidence, it is clear that all *Sturmstaffel* 1 aircraft appear to be either standard Fw 190 A-6 or A-7 variants fitted with four MG 151s. No evidence has so far been found that any Fw 190 A-7/R2 were actually delivered to the unit. It seems likely then that the A-7/R2s were primarily operated by the later *Sturmgruppen* of JG 3, JG 4 and JG 300 after *Sturmstaffel* 1 had been dissolved.

Fieseler works which started work on 10 machines in the first week of December 1943 followed by 20 the following week and 30 the third week. In all, it appears that Fieseler manufactured 60 Fw 190 A-7/R2s.

The standard A-7 variant production ran for a relatively short period, from November 1943 to February 1944, before being superseded by the Fw 190 A-8. This new variant had by far, the most number of modifications and sub-types, the most relevant for the *Sturmflugzeug* being the A-8/R2

This standard production Fw 190 A-8 is being delivered to a front-line unit. By this time, the 300 litre drop tank was a standard feature, but had been moved forward 200 mm to compensate for the extra fuel carried behind the cockpit.

Right and below *A pair of close-up pictures showing the port (to right) and starboard (below) views of a 300 litre drop tank attached to an ETC 501 carrier.*

Facsimilies and translations of original Focke-Wulf documents relating to this article can be found on pages 32-33 of this book.

Fw 190 / BMW 801

Jagdflugzeug

A-6
Änderungen.

Gegenüber A-5 (2MG 17, 2MG 151, 2MG FF)
2x MG 151 im Flügel anstelle MG FF)
Zellenseitige Vorbereitungen PuG 16 Z-B

Betriebstermin: Arado   Juni 1943
                Fieseler Juni 1943
                Ago   Juni 1943

Weiterentwicklung in der Serie:
Kühlerpanzeraufhängung. Neue Brücken (BSK 857) ab 16.8.43 in Serie
Später dir.Anfang.ab ca.Sept./Okt. 1943

A-6/R1   2x2MG151 unter d.Flügel.Umrüstung von 6o Flugz.von 1ZA Küpper
         bis 31.11.43 geliefert
A-6/R6   Anlage WGr 21 cm.   Nachrüstung durch ÄA Nr. 123 (auch A-5)
         Serieneinlauf ab Nov.1943 beginnend
         ab Febr.1944 100% der Serie

A-7
Änderungen :

Gegenüber A-6
a) 2MG131 anstelle MG17 im Rumpf
b) Vereinfachtes Bordnetz (Keine Abschirmung)
c) Revi 16b anstelle C12d
d) Vorbereitungen für Einheitssporn 380x150
   Jedoch für Jäger mit Rad 350x135

Betriebstermin: FW   Dez. 1943
                Ago   Nov. 1943
                Fieseler Nov. 1943

Sonderausführungen :

A-7/R2   2x1MK108 im Flügel   Fieseler
                                 Serieneinlauf: Des.43 10.2o,3o
A-7/R6   Anlage WGr 21 cm   Serieneinlauf: zu 5o% d.Flugz.

A-8
Änderungen :

a) Rumpfänderungen für wahlweise Einbaumöglichkeit
   eines GM-1-Anl.- oder 1151 Reichsweitenbehälters
b) FuG 16 Z-Y anstelle 16 Z (E) vorverlegt.
c) Rumpfbombenzusatz ETC 501 um 200 mm vorverlegt
d) Variometer.
e) WGr 21 cm-Anlage zelleneseitig eingebaut.

Betriebstermin: FW   Febr. 1944
                Ago   April 1944
                Fieseler Febr. 1944
                NDW   März 1944

A-8/R1   2x2MG151 unter d.Flügel.Für Serie aus Leistungsgründen am
         8.4.44 grundsätzlich entfallen.
A-8/R2   2x1MK108 im Flügel.   Fieseler
                                Serie ab ca. Febr. 44
A-8/R3   2x1MK103 unter d.Flügel siehe unter F-8/R3

GM 1-Anlage   Serie bei Ago für A-8/9 seit
                     31.7.44 nicht mehr gefordert.
Reichsweiten-Anlage Für alle Jäger gefordert
(1151)   Änderungsstufe 8/44

Kamera-Einbau   BSK 16-Anlage bis auf Kamera
                  einbauen.
                  Serieneinlauf: ca. Juni 1944
Erhöhte Notleistung Für alle Jäger gefordert.
                  Serieneinlauf: ab ca. Juni/Juli 44
Bastard-Triebwerk BMW 801 TU Triebwerk
                  D-Motor mit Triebwerksteilen
                  von TS/TH Triebwerk
                  als kompl. Wechseltriebwerk geliefert
                  voll austauschbar gegen 801 D-Triebwerk
                  (P600)

A-8/R11 Schlechtwetterjagd   Serieneinlauf: ca. Juli.
         mit 801 TU
                  a) Jägerkurssteuerung PKS 12
                  b) Heizscheiben
                  c) Notwendezeiger (nur ÄA)
                  d) FuG 125
                  Bauunterlagen: a,b) - 3.8.44
                                 c) ca.1.12.44
                                 d) 30.8.44
                  Serie:
                  a,b) ab September 44 FW
                  d) " November 44 FW

A-8/R8   Sturmflugzeuge   siehe unter A-9/R8
                  Diese Serie löst R2 ab.

Fw 190 / BMW 801

A-9
Änderungen :

Gegenüber A-8
a) Triebwerk BMW 801 TS/TH Leistungsgesteigert
   von BMW als kompl. Wechseltriebwerk geliefert
   voll austauschbar gegen 801 D Triebwerk (P600)
b) Neue Teile
   Schmierstoffkühler mit R8 2o (oder Überdruckventile)
   Panzerung für Kühler u.Ölbehälter verstärkt (1o u.6mm)
   Abgasanlage nur Einzeldüsen
                  Serieneinlauf: ca. Sept./Okt. 44 Beginn
                  je nach Lieferg.

A-9/R11 Schlechtwetterjagd   Ausrüstung wie A-8/R11
         mit 801 TS
A-9/R8   Sturmflugzeuge   Serie ca. Nov./Dez. 44
                  Zusätzl. Panzerung entfällt ab Jan. 45
                  Bewaffnung: 2MG 151 Flügelwurzel
                              2MK 108 Flügel außen
                  Serie: GFW   Dez.+Jan. 45
                         NDW   Febr.-März. 45
                         Arado ab Febr. 45

Focke-Wulf Flugzeugbau G.m.b.H.
Bad Eilsen

Techn. Zentrale   Datum: 21.3.1945

Fw 190 / BMW 801

Fighter Aircraft

A-6 Changes

Similar to A-5 (2MG 17, 2MG 151, 2MG FF)
2 x MG 151 in wing to replace MG FF
Airframe readiness to receive FuG 16 Z-E (radio set)

Tooling up completion:	Arado	June 1943
	Fieseler	June 1943
	Ago	June 1943

Further development of the series:

Armoured protection to cooler.		Gun camera installation
	New links (BSK 857) from 16.8.43 in series	BSK 16 equipment installed up to camera installation. Series production: around June 1944
	Later direct installation. From approx. Sept/Oct 1943	
A-6/R1 2 x 2MG 151 under the wing.	Conversion of 60 aircraft by LZA Küpper were delivered by 31.11.43	Increased emergency power	Proposed for all fighters Series production: from ca. June/July
A-6/R6 Installation of WGr 21 cm	Retro fitting of ÄA Nr. 123 (conversion pack No. 123) (also for A-5). Series production from beginning November 1943 from Feb.1944 100% of series	Bastard-Engine	BMW 801 TU Engine D-Engine containing engine parts from TS/TH engine. Engine delivered as complete interchangeable unit with the 801 D Engine (F600) Series production: around July 1944

A-7 Changes

Similar to A-6
a) 2MG 131 replacing the MG 17 in fuselage
b) Simplified Radio (no screening)
c) Revi 16b to replace C12d (gunsight)
d) Preparation to receive complete tailwheel assembly 380x150 also for fighters with wheels 350x135

Tooling up completion:	FW	Dec. 1943	All-weather fighter with 801 TU
	Ago	Nov. 1943	
	Fieseler	Nov. 1943	

A-8/R11

a) PKS 12 Autopilot
b) Heated windows
c) Emergency turn indicator (field installation only)
d) FuG 125 Radio

Special versions:

A-7/R2	2x1MK108 in wing	Fieseler Series production: Dec.4310,20,30	Construction details: a, b) - 3.8.44 c) around 1.12.44 d) 30.8.44 Series: a, b) from September 44 FW d) from November 44 FW
A-7/R6	Installation of WGr 21 cm	Series production: up to 50% of aircraft	

A-8/R8

Sturmflugzeug

See under A-9/R8
This series supersedes the R2

A-8 Changes

Similar to A-7
a) Fuselage changes to include the possibility of either one GM-1 (engine power booster) unit or 115 litre increase range fuel tank
b) FuG 16 Z-Y replacing 16Z (E) radio previously proposed
c) Fuselage bomb carrier ETC 501 moved 200 mm forward
d) Variometer
e) WGr 21 cm equipment installed into airframe

Tooling up completion:	FW	Feb. 1944	
	Ago	April 1944	
	Fieseler	Feb. 1944	
	NDW	March 1944	

A-9 Changes

Similar to A-8
a) Engine BMW 801 TS/TH with increased performance delivered by BMW as a complete interchangeable engine able to be completely exchanged for a 801 D engine (F600)
b) New parts
Lubrication cooler with Rö 20 (or high pressure vent)
Armour plating for cooler and oil tank increased (from 6 and 10mm)
Exhaust installation only single manifolds
Series production: around beginning Sept./Oct.44 each depending on delivery situation

A-8/R1	2x2MG151 under the wing	Due to reduction in performance, series production was discontinued on 8.4.44
A-8/R2	2x1MK108 in the wing	Series production from around Feb. 44 see under F-8/R3
A-8/R3	2x1MK103 under the wing	Series with AGO A-8/9 not necessary as from 31.7.44
	GM 1 equipment	

A-9/R11	All-weather fighter with 801 TS	Equipment as per A-8/R11 Series production around Nov./Dec.1944
A-9/R8	Sturmflugzeuge	Additional armour not fitted as from Jan.1945 Armament: 2MG 151 in wing root 2MK 108 outer wing

Increased range (115 litre tank)	Intended for all fighters and gradually introduced into production from 8/44

Series: GFW (Focke-Wulf)	Dec.+Jan.45
NDW (Nord Dornier Werk)	Feb.+Mar.45
Arado from Feb.45	

Focke-Wulf Flugzeugbau G.m.b.H.
Bad Eilsen

Techn. Zentrale

Datum: 21.3.1945

Left *Uffz. Werner Peinemann (left) of Sturmstaffel 1 sits in the cockpit of his Fw 190 whilst a mechanic leans over the 50 mm plate of strengthened frontal-plate glass. Note the 30 mm armoured glass quarter and side panels.*

Above *Three views showing the installation of the armoured glass panels – or Panzerscheiben – similar to those fitted around the standard glass cockpit side panels of the Fw 190 A-6s and A-7s of Sturmstaffel 1. Top right, shows the 50 mm plate of strengthened glass which would protect the pilot from fire from dead ahead, whilst centre and above show the 30 mm Thorax armoured glass side and quarter panels respectively, the former mounted in primitive rectangular wooden frames. These panels were designed to protect the Sturmstaffel pilots during their close range attacks against formations of USAAF four-engine bombers. Note in the photograph to above left, which shows Fw 190 A-8, W.Nr. 170397, the stencilled 'Starter Fuel 3 Litre' guide below the cockpit which first appeared on the A-8 variant.*

Left *A close up photograph showing a Fw 190 fitted with 5 mm steel plates to the fuselage panelling around the cockpit area which was intended to provide protection from defensive fire from USAAF heavy bombers.*

"After a year spent on the Russian front during 1942-43 and having specialised at the *Technische Schulen der Luftwaffe*, in October 1943, as an *Unteroffizier*, I was posted to *Sturmstaffel* 1 at Achmer along with several friends including Walter Stein, Franz X. Berger and Otto Altmeyer. *Sturmstaffel* 1 was forming up and needed specialists skilled on the BMW 801 engine and other mechanical aspects. So we came to know von Kornatzki and the unit's first pilots and we began to prepare and work on the Fw 190s as they arrived one by one."

"We were called 'M-Boys' – 'Maschine-Boys' – and were very close to *Major* von Kornatzki and his pilots. Von Kornatzki, *Major* Bacsila, as well as *Oberstabsarzt* Rübensaal were like fathers to us, always ready to help, including at times when our somewhat arrogant *Staffeldienstoffizier*, *Hptm.* Reinsperger, was out to make trouble for us."

"I can say that we considered these young men who were ready to ram, as real idols. This situation can only properly be understood by people who lived the way our people lived – feeling helpless to stop the bomber streams which came every day, terrorising our women, children and old people. I never imagined that such horror could have been possible. If I had had the occasion, I would also have become a *Rammjäger*. In fact, several weeks after my arrival at the *Sturmstaffel*, I asked von Kornatzki if I could become a ram-pilot. To my disappointment, he did not agree."

Their unit now fully equipped with personnel and aircraft, so a mood of impatience began to gnaw at the pilots of *Sturmstaffel* 1 as they waited for the next large-scale daylight raid and the opportunity to test both their courage and their tactics in combat.

Lt. Werner Gerth joined Sturmstaffel 1 in January 1944. He is seen here with a superimposed version of the Ritterkreuz he was awarded on 29 October 1944 whilst Staffelkapitän of 14.(Sturm)/JG 3. He was killed four days later having reportedly rammed a B-17 north of Bitterfeld.

Wednesday, 5 January 1944

On the morning of 5 January, the German early warning system reported the assembly of large American formations over England. Just like the day before – which marked the first daylight attack against a German target in the New Year – Kiel was to be the target. Escorted by 70 P-38 Lightnings, 119 B-17 Flying Fortresses of the 1st Bombardment Division and 96 B-24 Liberators of the 2nd Bombardment Division set out to bomb the city's shipyards. The visual attack enabled a good concentration of bombs to hit their assigned target.

But the way to the target was not without adversity. At 10.00 hrs, the first German fighters were scrambled to intercept. However, *Sturmstaffel* 1 – together with I./JG 1 and II./JG 27 – was kept on the ground for another two hours. When these units did finally take-off, it was the more experienced pilots of I./JG 1 who met the first elements of the bomber formation over Belgium at 12.45 hrs scoring one victory and four B-17 *Herausschüsse*. The *Gruppe* paid a heavy price, losing three of its pilots killed.

It was to prove an inauspicious start for *Sturmstaffel* 1; the unit made no contact with the enemy and returned to Dortmund.

Lack of operational success did not dampen spirits however. *Lt.* Hans Berger, a pilot with I./JG 1 recalled: "Our I./JG 1 had been in Dortmund since mid December. Early in January, *Sturmstaffel* 1 arrived at the airfield and it was not long before a grand parade was held comprising the pilots of both JG 1 and the *Sturmstaffel*. We were inspected by *Oberst* Grabmann, commander of 3. *Jagddivision*, and *Major* von Kornatzki. It was probably on this occasion that we were briefed on the concept of the *Sturmjäger*. It was all done in a very colourful and positive way; they would be able to shoot down a lot of bombers by using a method that was considered more efficient than ours. They would fly close to the bombers and attack from behind. This was completely different to what we did. We attacked head on."

"We were given some time to think about whether we wanted to join the *Sturmstaffel*, but, in spite of the optimistic picture they painted, we were convinced that this type of attack was almost suicidal and not one of our pilots showed any enthusiasm for the idea. In fact, not a single pilot from the *Gruppe* volunteered."

Lt. Hans Berger (right) of I./JG 1 poses for a snapshot with his chief mechanic and ground crew. Berger remembers being given the opportunity to volunteer for the Sturmstaffel but declined because he – along with other pilots of his Gruppe – considered the unit's tactics to be "...almost suicidal."

The first B-17 to be shot down by Sturmstaffel 1 fell to the guns of Oblt. Othmar Zehart on 11 January 1944. He is seen here in the cockpit of Fw 190 A-6 'White 7'. Note the cockpit side armour, but lack of armoured glass panels for the canopy.

The 94th Bomb Group's B-17 Frenesi parked safely on a rain-dampened dispersal at Bury St. Edmunds, England following its return to base from the 11 January mission to Germany during which Sturmstaffel 1 registered its first 'kill' over a B-17. Here Frenesi's pilot, 2nd Lt. William Cely from Houston Texas and her co-pilot, 2nd Lt. Jabez F. Churchill from Santa Rosa, California survey the damage inflicted on their aircraft by German fighters. Despite battle damage to the tail, wings and one of the engines, as well as a failed oxygen and intercom system, Frenesi made it back, testimony to the resilience of the Flying Fortress.

Lt. Richard Franz of Sturmstaffel 1 recalls: "At that time Sturmstaffel 1 was the only unit which attacked the Viermots from the rear and all the other pilots who flew in the Reichsverteidigung thought we were a little bit crazy. They all preferred to attack head on with the advantages and disadvantages that came with it. The Sturmstaffel pilots on the other hand, voluntarily bound themselves to bring down one bomber per engagement, either with their weapons or by ramming. I never had to ram, thank God."

Tuesday, 11 January 1944

The pattern of American bombing throughout January 1944 was dictated to a great extent by prevailing overcast weather conditions over north-west Europe which necessitated pathfinder-led missions against German ports and industrial areas. The only major visual operation occurred on 11 January when the weather was expected to be fine. The weather however was to prove fickle and the American bomber force of 663 aircraft pushed on in deteriorating conditions to hit several aviation and industrial targets in the heart of the Reich – Oschersleben, Halberstadt, Braunschweig and Osnabrück – on a mission which was to mark the commencement of "Operation Pointblank", the strategic air offensive against Germany designed to bring about "the progressive destruction and dislocation of the German military and economic system".

In readiness, Sturmstaffel 1 and I./JG 1 transferred from Dortmund to Rheine and waited for the order to take-off. It came at 10.30. Thirty minutes later, I./JG 1 executed a frontal attack against the American formation and shot down three bombers in as many minutes between 11.08 and 11.10. The Sturmstaffel separated from I./JG 1 and, in conformity with its intended tactical doctrine, attacked an American combat-box from the rear. Approaching at close range, Oblt. Othmar Zehart opened fire simultaneously with the other pilots of the Staffel and scored the first kill – a B-17 – for his unit.

The following days saw the weather close in and deteriorate still further, bringing a temporary respite from the bombing of German targets. Despite the seemingly endless and nerve-jangling waiting, morale in the *Sturmstaffel* was not affected. An example of this can be found in a letter which *Uffz.* Heinz von Neuenstein wrote to his father:

Dortmund, 17 January 1944

Dear Father,

Actually I did not want to write to you until I had a kill. The Americans are not coming, partly because of the weather and partly because of the setback they suffered on January 11th. It will be a long time before we are sent into action again and so I don't want to wait that long in order to write to you.

On the above mentioned day, I was in action and fired into the bomber formation. That is all I did. Now I shall be able to make up for such a cock-up. You really can't imagine how badly I feel about something like that, especially if it takes such a long time to get the opportunity to make up for it. One thing I can promise you; I shall not come back without two kills unless my engine is hit. I have made up my mind and I shall not fail. It would be intolerable for me to know that members of my unit have more victories than I do. Such a thing is unthinkable. If it is possible, I want to bring down three; shoot down the first two and ram the third.

If it turns out badly, then I have done my duty and have fulfilled the rules of my unit, which is unique in Germany. May God grant me the strength at the decisive moment to carry out this mission. If only the opportunity would come soon! This waiting is unbearable. You should experience this waiting for action for three years, and then still have to sit around!

Uffz. Heinz von Neuenstein. "One thing I can promise you: I shall not come back without two kills unless my engine is hit."

Saturday, 29 January 1944

With the exception of an ultimately aborted large-scale raid planned against Frankfurt-am-Main on the 24th, bad weather temporarily halted Eighth Air Force raids over German territory until 29 January. The *Sturmstaffel's* pilots used the short respite for practice missions and tactical planning.

On the 29th, the Americans came again, this time dispatching 863 B-17s and B-24s to targets in the Frankfurt area. Escorted by 632 fighters, a record 806 bombers dropped more than 1,895 tons of bombs over the primary target and the escorts shot down 44 *Luftwaffe* fighters between 11.00-13.05 hrs along the route over France, Belgium and Germany.

At 10.25 hrs, 16 Fw 190s of I./JG 1, possibly supported by aircraft from *Sturmstaffel* 1, took off from Dortmund to intercept, but made no contact with the enemy.

Sunday, 30 January 1944

Continuing its "Pointblank" goal of "undermining the morale of the German people to a point where their capacity for armed resistance is fatally weakened", the Eighth Air Force launched a force of 777 heavy bombers against aircraft manufacturing plants around Braunschweig and Hannover. Escorted by 635 USAAF fighters, the bombers were again forced to bomb through cloud.

At 11.45 hrs, I./JG 1 accompanied by *Sturmstaffel* 1 made contact with a large formation of *Viermots* south west of Osnabrück. The *Sturmstaffel* separated from the main German force and closed in on a formation of B-24 Liberators, probably the 39 aircraft of the 1st Combat Wing which had diverted towards Hannover due to dense smoke and contrails encountered over Braunschweig.

One Liberator fell to the guns of *Uffz.* Willi Maximowitz around 11.50 hrs, and in conformity with the oath he had taken, *Uffz.* Hermann Wahlfeld rammed another, remarkably without any injury to himself.

Uffz. Hermann Wahlfeld is reported to have rammed a B-24 on 30 January 1944.

Major Erwin Bacsila jumps from the cockpit of his Fw 190 A-6 following a mission on 30 January 1944 during which he claimed the destruction of a B-17. Note the cockpit side armour, armoured glass 'blinkers' fitted to the canopy and the Sturmstaffel 1 emblem applied to the aircraft's cowling.

Major Erwin Bacsila also claimed the destruction of a B-17, not a B-24 like his fellow pilots, an indication that the *Sturmstaffel* had become broken up during the action.

I./JG 1 reported the destruction of seven B-17s for the loss of three pilots. *Sturmstaffel* 1 suffered the loss of *Fhr.* Manfred Derp from defensive fire west of Osnabrück and also, in a cruel irony, *Uffz.* Heinz von Neuenstein, who had promised his father that he would "do his duty" in his letter of a few days before.

Lt. Ulrich Blaese was wounded and was forced to bale out of his Fw 190 near Diepholz. It would be a long time before Blaese was fit for operations again.

Elsewhere, *Uffz.* Werner Peinemann suffered burns to his face and hands before taking to his parachute not far from Sachsenhagen. Unlike Blaese however, Peinemann was back in action within a few weeks.

These early battle experiences, combined with the highly hazardous nature of their work, may have served as the motivation behind some *Sturmstaffel* pilots experimenting with the wearing of steel infantry helmets as a form of additional armour protection during the initial period of operations. Oscar Boesch, who did not join the *Sturmstaffel* until April 1944, remembers what his fellow pilots told him: "It, not surprisingly, proved impractical. Wearing a steel helmet in the cockpit resulted in the complete inability of the pilot to move his head when in combat!"

The idea was soon abandoned.

At least two pilots – Heinz Birkigt and Rudolf Pancherz – were posted from the *Sturmstaffel* to 3./JG 11 at the end of January 1944. Birkigt claimed six victories with JG 11 before being killed in action as a *Feldwebel* on 25 August 1944 during operations on the Invasion Front, whilst Pancherz made one claim before being killed on 3 March 1944 in a mid-air collision with another pilot from his unit.

Besides the four total aircraft losses incurred, 11 other Fw 190s were damaged during the attack on 30 January, resulting in a catastrophic 60% aircraft loss and damage rate for the *Staffel* at the end of its first month of operations.

Sturmstaffel 1 Victories – January 1944

Date	Pilot	Aircraft	Time
11-01-44	Oblt. Othmar Zehart	B-17 (1)	
30-01-44	Uffz. Willi Maximowitz	B-24 (1)	11.50 (approx.)
	Uffz. Hermann Wahlfeld	B-24 (1)	11.50 (approx.)
	Major Erwin Bacsila	B-17 (34?)	11.50

Sturmstaffel 1 Losses – January 1944

Date	Pilot	Aircraft		
30/01/44	Fhr. Manfred Derp (KIA)	Fw 190 A-6 550920) White 11	100%	in combat Nordel near Hannover
30/01/44	Uffz. Heinz von Neuenstein (KIA)	Fw 190 A-6 (550978) White 6	100%	in combat Berber/ Bad Münder
30/01/44	Lt. Ulrich Blaese (WIA)	Fw 190 A-6 (550779)	? %	in combat near Diepholz
30/01/44	Lt. Werner Peinemann (WIA)	Fw 190 A-6	? %	parachuted after combat near Sachsenhagen

Fhr. Manfred Derp, who joined Sturmstaffel 1 from JG 26, was killed in action over Osnabrück on 30 January 1944.

```
                  A b s c h r i f t !
Der Reichsminister der Luftfahrt        Berlin, den 9.6.1944
und Oberbefehlshaber der Luftwaffe
Luftwaffenpersonalamt
Az.29 Nr.    132    /44 ((A)5., V)


             An    Sturmstaffel 1

     Der    Sturmstaffel 1

wird der Abschuss eines    amerikanischen Kampfflugzeuges vom
Typ Boeing "Fortress II"        am 30.1.44        11.50 Uhr

durch Major  B a c s i l a

als  e r s t e r    (1.)  Luftsieg der Staffel anerkannt.

                            I.A.
                            Unterschrift

F.d.R.d.A.
O.U., den 15.10.44


        Leutnant und Offz.z.b.V.
```

Left *The confirmation certificate of Major Erwin Bacsila's victory over a B-17 on 30 January 1944*

Above *Following the succesful completion of Sturmstaffel 1's first operation from Dortmund in mid-Janauary 1944, Major Erwin Bacsila (left) poses for the camera on the wing of Fw 190 A-6 'White 7' and allows one of his mechanics to sit in the 'hot seat'.*

Above *Major Erwin Bacsila (right) describes the events of the Sturmstaffel's first mission from Dortmund to his ground crew, mid-January 1944. This photograph clearly shows the cockpit side armour and armoured glass quarter-panels and side 'blinkers' fitted to the cockpit of Fw 190 A-6 'White 7'.*

Major Erwin Bacsila reports to Major von Kornatzki on the outcome of the Sturmstaffel's first mission from Dortmund against American heavy bombers, January 1944. From its overall condition, the Fw 190 A-6 seen in the background appears to be freshly delivered to the unit.

Major Hans-Günter von Kornatzki (far right) prepares his pilots for an inspection at Dortmund by Oberst Walter Grabmann, the Kommandeur of 3. Jagddivision. The 3. Jagddivision, headquartered at Deelen in Holland, assumed overall tactical control of all fighter Gruppen based throughout north-west Germany, Holland and parts of Belgium. Behind the Sturmstaffel pilots can be seen one of the units Fw 190 A-6s adorned with the lightning and gauntlet unit badge on the cowling and the black-white-black fuselage identification band. Also visible is the armoured glass 'blinker' mounted to the side of the canopy. Standing in the foreground is Hptm. Alfred Grislawski, Staffelkapitän of 1./JG 1.

Right and below
Accompanied by Major von Kornatzki and Hptm. Alfred Grislawski, Staffelkapitän of 1./JG 1, Oberst Grabmann addresses Sturmstaffel 1 on the rain-slick apron at Dortmund. Grabmann was a veteran of the Legion Condor's campaign during the Spanish Civil War and later commanded ZG 76 before taking up regional command positions.

From left to right, unknown, Ofw. Gerhard Marburg, Uffz. Kurt Röhrich, Uffz. Werner Peinemann, and Gefr. Gerhard Vivroux listen attentively as Major von Kornatzki explains the development and operations of his Staffel to Oberst Grabmann at Dortmund.

The lightning and gauntlet badge of Sturmstaffel 1 seen on the cowling of an Fw 190 at either Dortmund or Salzwedel in 1944. According to former members of the unit, the clenched gauntlet represents the specially-fitted armour as found on the unit's aircraft, whilst the lightning bolt symbolises the speed and ferocity of an attack by the Sturmstaffel on a formation of bombers.

Pilots from Sturmstaffel 1 push one of their
Fw 190 A-6s back to its dispersal, 'encouraged' by
Major Erwin Bacsila.

An Fw 190 A-6 of Sturmstaffel 1 runs up its engine. Probably taken at Dortmund in early 1944, the aircraft carries the unit's large lightning and gauntlet unit badge on its cowling and has been fitted with armoured glass quarter-panels and side 'blinkers'. Note also the black and white identification bands on the fuselage.

4. DEFENDING THE FATHERLAND

Thursday, 10 February 1944

By now, more experienced pilots had reached the *Sturmstaffel*, including *Lt.* Richard Franz who had arrived from the Mediterranean theatre where he had been flying with 3./JG 77. Before that, Franz had seen service with JG 27 in Africa, followed by a spell with the *Ergängzungs Jagdgruppe Süd* in southern France. He recalled at the time: "At the end of 1943, when I was serving as a pilot with JG 77 in Italy, I heard about a request from the *Reichsmarschall* for volunteers for a new unit for the Defence of the Reich. Although we were in action far from home, we knew that the situation there was precarious and that the air raids were becoming more frequent and more destructive. I volunteered without knowing what to expect, other than I would be in action against four-engined bombers. I reported to my commander who sent the transfer request to Berlin. At the end of January/beginning of February, I was transferred to *Sturmstaffel* 1. I took the train to Dortmund by myself, (none of the other pilots from my unit had volunteered), only to find out that my unit had been transferred. So I made my way to Salzwedel, where I reported to *Major* von Kornatzki. It was from him that I first heard what was expected from a *Sturmjäger*. He was very kind and I still have a good impression of him. He suggested that I think about my decision before I finally made up my mind. I returned to my fellow pilots and I can testify that none was in any way what you would call a fanatic. They had all based their decision on the need to defend the Fatherland and the civilian population from the bombers. More than in any other units, the emphasis here is to fly in tight formation. Our tactics consist of a tight 'V'-formation on approach and an attack from behind. Von Kornatzki does not fly with us very often because he is in poor health. Most of our sorties are led by *Lt.* Gerth who has the most kills."

> **"By the end of March, the Commander-in-Chief of the Luftwaffe was less worried about the development of the air war situation over the Reich than he had been during February... It was evident that the success of our defense operations during the enemy attacks on Berlin contributed to this feeling on his part..."**
>
> *Generalleutnant a.D. Josef Schmid, The Employment of the German Luftwaffe against the Allies in the West, 1943-1945*
> *USAF Historical Studies Nos. 158-160*

Early in the morning of 10 February, *Sturmstaffel* 1 together with I./JG 1 transferred to Rheine and awaited further operational orders. This was always a tense, nerve-wracking time for the German pilots, as Richard Franz recalls: "Although the Allies had gained air superiority in 1943, I think that the morale of our fighter pilots was not bad, especially when it is realised that the young pilots we had in the front-line units had very little experience and a life expectancy of something like 10 missions. It was a hard time for both the young pilots as well as for their leaders."

"Normally, we were informed at about 07.00 hrs of a "*grosse Versammlung*" – a large enemy assembly – over Great Yarmouth. After breakfast, we were driven to the *Staffel's* dispersal and then had 30 minutes readiness. About 45 minutes before the expected take-off and after determination of the probable target area, cockpit readiness was ordered until finally, the scramble order was given. After scramble, all units were ordered to meet at a certain point and then form up into a battle formation – sometimes up to 100 aircraft – before being directed to a pre-assigned attack

Lt. Richard Franz.

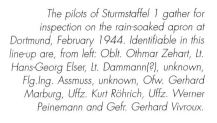

The pilots of Sturmstaffel 1 gather for inspection on the rain-soaked apron at Dortmund, February 1944. Identifiable in this line-up are, from left: Oblt. Othmar Zehart, Lt. Hans-Georg Elser, Lt. Dammann(?), unknown, Flg.Ing. Assmuss, unknown, Ofw. Gerhard Marburg, Uffz. Kurt Röhrich, Uffz. Werner Peinemann and Gefr. Gerhard Vivroux.

position from where we would separate from the main formation for our rearward attack. The main formation would always try to overtake the bomber stream in order to get into position for a head-on attack."

At 10.30 hrs, *Sturmstaffel* 1 and I./JG 1 took off and, together with II./JG 1, were directed to attack the 169 B-17 Flying Fortresses of the 3rd Bomb Division heading for the aircraft plants around Braunschweig. Though the bombers were protected by 466 P-38, P-47 and P-51 fighters, the day would see some of the hardest-fought air combat ever to take place over north-west Europe.

Under the overall leadership of the veteran *Experte* and *Ritterkreuzträger*, Major Heinz Bär, the German fighters hit the bombers north of Osnabrück. Thirteen B-17s were claimed as brought down by JG 1 as well as one *Herausschuss* and four P-47 Thunderbolts, for the loss of two pilots.

Successes for the *Sturmstaffel* were still proving to be hard-won and the unit claimed only one victory, when a B-17 was shot down by *Ofhr.* Heinz Steffen at 7,500 m (24,606 ft) near Rheine. There were no losses.

The final losses incurred by the Eighth Air Force following the Braunschweig mission were considered "unsustainable." In all, 295 crewmen and 29 bombers were listed as missing – 20 per cent of the force.

The photographs below were taken at the same time as the one above and in the left hand picture Uffz. Willi Maximowitz can be seen behind Vivroux and Peinemann.

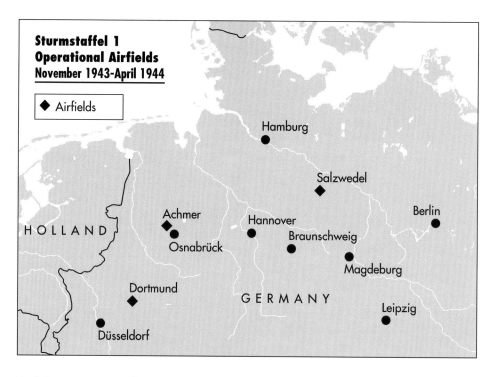

Friday, 11 February 1944

With only 7 serviceable Fw 190s and operating on its own, *Sturmstaffel* 1 attacked B-17s of the 1st Bomb Division on their way to bomb marshalling yards at Frankfurt-am-Main. Breaking through the escort, *Flg.* Wolfgang Kosse demonstrated his experience by shooting down one Flying Fortress at 12.35 hrs and five minutes later, *Ofhr.* Heinz Steffen did likewise. The unit lost one aircraft.

Around this time, *Sturmstaffel* 1 took delivery of the Fw 190 A-7, a variant of the Focke-Wulf fighter which had been put into production in December 1943. The A-7 featured simplified electrics, improved radio, stronger mainwheel hubs and the new Revi 16B gunsight. As far as armament was concerned, it was intended that the A-7

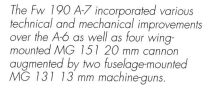

The Fw 190 A-7 incorporated various technical and mechanical improvements over the A-6 as well as four wing-mounted MG 151 20 mm cannon augmented by two fuselage-mounted MG 131 13 mm machine-guns.

would incorporate four wing-mounted MG 151s augmented by two fuselage-mounted MG 131 13 mm machine-guns, these being belt-fed air-cooled weapons weighing only 18 kg (40 lb) each, capable of firing 960 rounds per minute and housed in 'bulges' directly in front of the cockpit. These 'bulges' were necessitated by the size of the gun and became a distinguishing characteristic of the Fw 190 A-7 and later variants.

However, the A-7s completed by Fieseler appeared as Fw 190 A-7/R2s, aircraft fitted with two wing-mounted 30 mm MK 108 cannon which replaced the outboard MG 151s. By early April 1944, *Sturmstaffel* 1 is known to have had at least four such aircraft on strength.

The prime benefit of the MK 108, used profusely by the *Luftwaffe* for close-range anti-bomber work over north-west and southern Europe, lay in its simplicity and economic process of manufacture, the greater part of its components consisting of pressed sheet metal stampings. Its operation bore similarities to the Becker-Oerlikon method as used during the closing months of the First World War and into the 1930s and in many ways, the MK 108 was considered to have been a masterpiece in weapons engineering, not only saving precious materials but also hundreds of man hours on milling machines and precision grinders.

With the advent of massed American daylight bomber formations bristling with concentrated defensive firepower, the need arose for a long-range, heavy calibre gun with which a German pilot could target specific bombers, expend the least amount of ammunition, score a kill in the shortest possible time and yet stay beyond the range of the defensive guns. It was a virtually impossible requirement and yet the MK 108 almost achieved this, though at first the *Techisches Amt* of the RLM rejected Rheinmetall's first proposal on the basis that German fighter pilots were considered by Ernst Udet, the *Generalluftzeugmeister*, all to be crack-shots easily capable of shooting down the heaviest bomber with 20 mm calibre weapons at extended ranges!

First designed in 1940 by Rheinmetall-Borsig, one of Germany's leading arms manufacturers, as a private venture, the MK 108 was a blow-back operated, rear-seared, belt-fed cannon, using electric ignition, being charged and triggered by compressed air, though once installed into any aircraft, there was no method of adjustment for harmonisation. One of the most unusual physical features of the gun was its extremely short barrel earning it the type-name *Kurzgerät* (lit. 'short apparatus') and which gave it its low muzzle velocity of between 500-540 m (1640-1770 ft) per second with a maximum rate of fire of 650 rounds per minute. At only half the weight of the MK 103 wing-mounted cannon, two MK 108s represented the same payload but had a combined rate of fire slightly more than three times that of a single MK 103. The weapon was subsequently integrated into the later variants of the Bf 109 and the Fw 190 A-8 where it quickly earned a fearsome reputation amongst Allied bomber crews who dubbed it the "pneumatic hammer".

Lt. Richard Franz of *Sturmstaffel* 1 remembers using the MK 108 in action against B-17s: "When we made our final attack, we approached from slightly above, then dived, and opened fire with 13 mm and 20 mm guns to knock out the rear gunner and then, at about 150 m, we tried to engage with the MK 108, which really was a terrible weapon. It was able to cut the wing of a B-17 off. Actually,

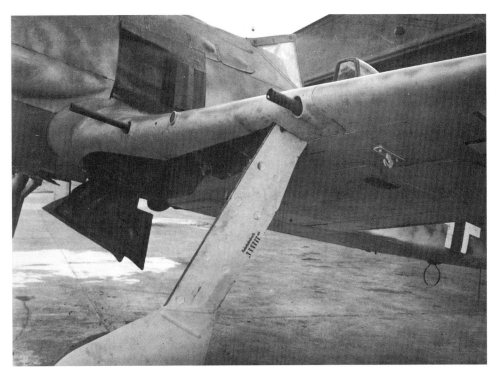

This Fw 190 A-6, W.Nr. 530765 TG+AT, was built by Fiesler and was the first aircraft converted to carry the 30 mm MK 108 cannon installed in the wing.

The MK 108 30 mm cannon.

Above Uffz. Willi Maximowitz (left) and Gefr. Gerhard Vivroux smile at the camera from Fw 190 A-6 'White 2' outside the hangar at Dortmund in early 1944. Clearly visible are the armoured glass side panel fitted to the aircraft's canopy and the large gauntlet and lightning emblem of Sturmstaffel 1 adorning the machine's cowling.

Above Gerhard Vivroux (right) stands for a photograph by Fw 190 A-6 'White 2' with Gefr. Franz X. Berger (left in white overalls) and another unidentified member of Sturmstaffel 1 at Dortmund, early 1944.

Right Uffz. Kurt Röhrich (left) Uffz. Werner Peinemann (centre) and Uffz. Willi Maximowitz share a joke outside the hanger at Dortmund, 1944

it was still easier to kill a B-24 which was somewhat weaker in respect of fuselage strength and armament. I think that we generally had the better armament and ammunition, whereas the other side had the better aircraft."

Two basic types of shells could be loaded into the MK 108; the 30 mm high explosive self-destroying tracer type 'M-Shell' designed to cause blast effect and the 30 mm high explosive self-destroying incendiary shell intended to cause both a blast and incendiary effect. German weapons and ballistics technicians at Rheinmetall-Borsig's main testing ground at Unterlüss in consultation with the *Luftwaffe's* principal *Erprobungsstelle* at Rechlin, had decided that the maximum destruction to an enemy aircraft could be created by causing the largest possible explosive effect in its interior, but that this in turn was dictated by the size of the enemy aircraft and by the quantity of explosive that could physically be placed into a projectile. The thicker the shell wall, the more energy was needed for the destruction of the shell itself and thus, less energy remained for the destruction of the target by the ensuing explosion. This theory led to the development of the 'Mine Shell' which combined a minimum thickness in shell casing with a maximum load of explosive. Using such ammunition, the entire enemy aircraft could be regarded as the 'target area', it making no difference where the hit was actually made. As such, with 'Mine Shells' a fighter pilot had an inherently greater chance of scoring a kill.

Following tests carried out at Rechlin, it was discovered that five hits from a 30 mm 'M-Shell' carrying 85 g of explosive were needed for the destruction of either a B-17 Flying Fortress or B-24 Liberator.

Conversely however, incendiary shells were also considered an extremely potent form of ammunition but only really effective when they hit fuel tanks. In such a case, therefore, the vulnerability of an enemy aircraft could be measured by the area/size of its tanks. However, a certain degree of penetrative force was still needed in order to break through the airframe or any protective armour carried by the target without breaking up and igniting until actually striking the fuel. To overcome this problem, the 30 mm incendiary shell was fitted with a hydrodynamic fuse which activated only when making contact with a fluid.

When attacked by a fighter directly from behind, the area of a B-17 Flying Fortress taken up by its fuel tanks was approximately 1/5 of the total and it was assumed that by the time an attack was made the tanks would be half empty. Thus, in combat conditions, this area was reduced to 1/10 of surface area. It was calculated that between five and ten 30 mm incendiary shells were needed to cause inextinguishable burning. However, in the case of attacking B-24 Liberators, an effective attack using incendiaries was slightly more difficult since the bomber's main fuel tanks were located in the fuselage with only reserve tanks located in the wings behind the engines.

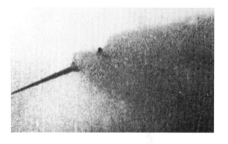

Camera gun records showing the destruction of B-17 Flying Fortresses by German fighter attack.

Monday, 21 February 1944

Prompted by General "Hap" Arnold's directive the previous Christmas to "... destroy the enemy air force wherever you find them; in the air, on the ground, and in the factories...", the Eighth Air Force launched "Operation Argument" or "Big Week", a concerted and intensive bombing campaign against German aircraft production centres, specifically against the principal airframe, final assembly and component plants responsible for the output of single- and twin-engine fighters such as those at Leipzig-Mockau, Halberstadt and Regensburg. In all, 16 Combat Wings of heavy bombers, comprising 1,000 aircraft were committed to the operation, together with fighter protection from all available groups of both the Eighth and Ninth Air Forces. It was to be the largest force ever assembled in the history of American strategic airpower.

The mission to the aircraft plants on the 20th marked the commencement of "Big Week" and the following day, the 21st, the targets for a force of 762 bombers and nearly 700 fighters were airfields ranged across central and north west Germany.

Luftwaffe reaction to this raid was apparently ineffective, for the Eighth Air Force reported: *"Enemy air opposition was remarkably weak considering the depth of penetration and the importance to the Luftwaffe of targets attacked. Enemy formations*

Right *Uffz. Walter Köst of Sturmstaffel 1 was killed in action in his Fw 190 A-7 on 21 February 1944 near Lübecke.*

Far right *Uffz. Erich Lambertus was killed in action in his Fw 190 A-7 on 21 February 1944. He had been one of the Sturmstaffel's earliest volunteers.*

were small and scattered, attacks more sporadic..." Nevertheless, the *Sturmstaffel* took on the Americans over northern Germany. At 15.00, *Uffz.* Kurt Röhrich claimed a B-17. Fifteen minutes later, *Fw.* Gerhard Marburg shot down another, following this with a *Herausschuss* ten minutes after that.

However, the *Staffel* did suffer losses over Lübeck when *Uffz.* Erich Lambertus was killed in action in his Fw 190 A-7 'White 3', 25 km (15.5 mls) north east of the city and *Uffz.* Walter Köst was hit and killed over Sundern.

Tuesday, 22 February 1944

The third day of the "Big Week" offensive, saw the first co-ordinated operation mounted against German targets by the Eighth and Fifteenth Air Forces striking from the west and south respectively. For 289 B-17s of the Eighth's 1st Bomb Division, the targets included aircraft plants at Aschersleben, Bernburg, Halberstadt and Magdeburg.

Lt. Werner Gerth of *Sturmstaffel* 1 prevented one bomber from returning to England when he shot it down at 13.40 hrs. The unit incurred no losses.

General Henry H. "Hap" Arnold, (left), Commanding General of the USAAF, chats to American bomber crewmen at a base somewhere in England. In December 1943, Arnold ordered the forces under his command to "... destroy the enemy air force wherever you find them; in the air, on the ground, and in the factories...".

Saturday, 26 February 1944

The *Sturmstaffel* transferred to its new base at Salzwedel, some 200 km (125 mls) west of Berlin, staging via Hannover-Langenhagen.

With ten operational machines available, the unit was assigned to IV./JG 3 which had also just arrived at Salzwedel from Venlo in Holland. Formed at Neubiberg in June 1943 and equipped with the Bf 109 G-6, IV./JG 3 had seen action against USAAF heavy bombers over Sicily and southern Italy between July and September of that year, under the command of *Ritterkreuzträger*, *Hptm.* Franz Beyer. Some of its aircraft had been the first to be fitted with 21 cm WGr. under-wing air-to-air mortars designed to be fired into bomber *Pulks* so as to break up a formation and its defensive firepower. However, as the Allies doggedly advanced up through Italy in September 1943, the *Gruppe* was forced to pull back from its

base at Cassano, firstly to Bari and then to San Severo from where, due to the approach of the British Eighth Army and pressing requirements in the Reich, it was withdrawn to Germany.

Following a short spell at Neubiberg, the *Gruppe* was moved to Venlo and Grimbergen in Holland for defensive operations in the West. On 11 February, Beyer was killed following an engagement purportedly with RAF Spitfires over Venlo. His place was taken by another *Ritterkreuzträger*, *Major* Friedrich Karl Müller, the former *Gruppenkommandeur* of I./JG 53.

Personal baggage belonging to the pilots of Sturmstaffel 1 is unloaded from a transport glider on a wintry day at Salzwedel following the unit's arrival there from Dortmund at the end of February 1944. Seen in the picture to left, Uffz. Gerhard Vivroux (left) and Uffz. Willi Maximowitz (second from left) help to sort the cases. Note the Fw 190 in the picture to right with its distinctive black-white-black fuselage bands.

Wednesday, 1 March 1944

The new month opened with *Sturmstaffel* 1 reporting the loss of *Uffz.* Heinz Grosskreuz following an attempted emergency landing near Uelzen whilst on a transfer flight. It was to be a sad day for Rudolf Fendt, his mechanic, who remembers: "The pilot with whom I was most closely linked was 'my pilot', *Uffz.* Grosskreuz. Grosskreuz came from East Prussia and was an extremely good pilot, incredibly gifted and I think the best in our *Staffel*. We immediately became friends and he knew that he would be able to trust me under all circumstances. Of course, we spoke about his reasons for joining such a dangerous unit. He told me about his personal reasons; several members of his family had been killed as a result of the war. Nevertheless, he wanted to do the best for his country and his personal circumstances allowed him to take the risk.

I remember that at the end of a particular mission, we were anxiously waiting for the return of our pilots. When the *Staffel* had landed, it was realised that Grosskreuz was missing. I was very worried but about fifteen minutes later, I recognised the sound of 'my' aircraft. He passed over the airfield shaking his wings, passed again and shook them for a second time. That meant he had claimed two victories. When he landed, we discovered that he had been wounded. Nevertheless, he was congratulated and presented with two bottles of champagne. This practice of awarding bottles of champagne would continue and, when a large part of our *Staffel* was incorporated into IV.(*Sturm*)/JG 3 and sent to France after the Invasion, the champagne was replaced by cognac! It helped to maintain morale!"

"Grosskreuz became *Lt.* Gerth's *Rottenflieger*. Both pilots enjoyed a firm friendship but there was also an element of competition, Gerth,

Upon moving to Salzwedel, Sturmstaffel 1 was assigned to IV./JG 3 which had previously seen service in the Mediterranean. Here one of that unit's Bf 109 G-6/R2s is seen at its dispersal in southern Italy. This variant was fitted with two 21 cm WGr mortar tubes under the wing.

Sturmstaffel 1 emblem

Fw 190 A-6 'White 5' Sturmstaffel 1, Dortmund early 1944

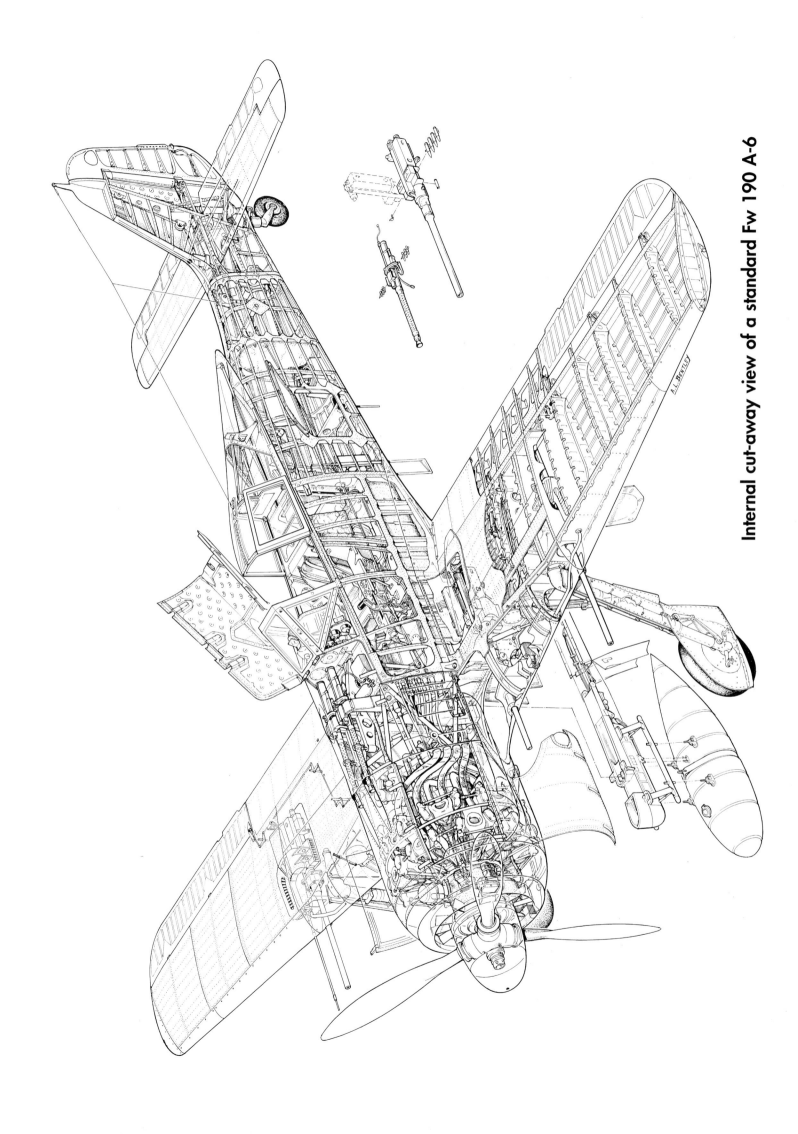

Internal cut-away view of a standard Fw 190 A-6

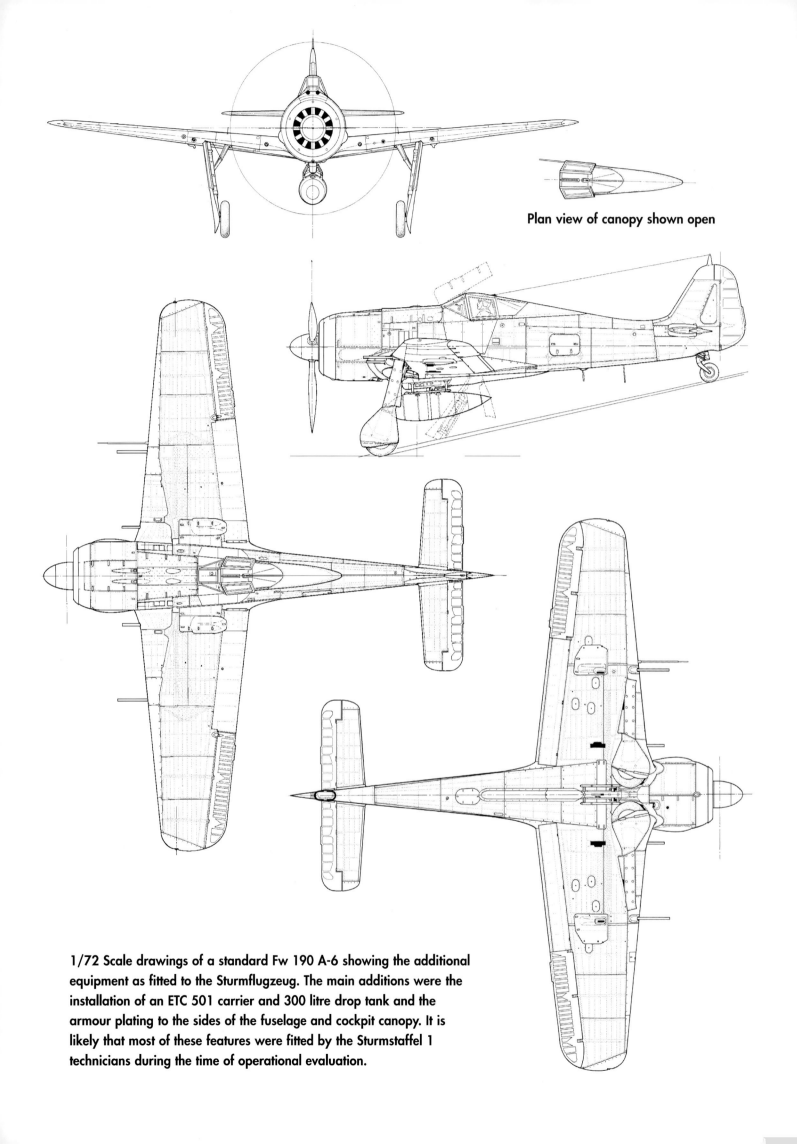

Plan view of canopy shown open

1/72 Scale drawings of a standard Fw 190 A-6 showing the additional equipment as fitted to the Sturmflugzeug. The main additions were the installation of an ETC 501 carrier and 300 litre drop tank and the armour plating to the sides of the fuselage and cockpit canopy. It is likely that most of these features were fitted by the Sturmstaffel 1 technicians during the time of operational evaluation.

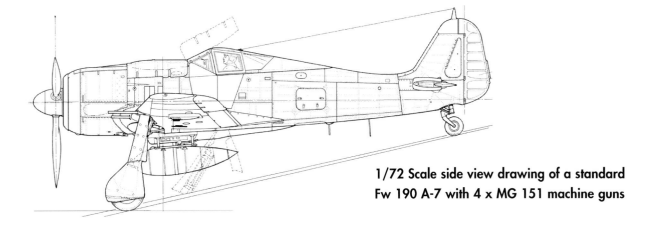

1/72 Scale side view drawing of a standard
Fw 190 A-7 with 4 x MG 151 machine guns

Original handbook drawing showing armament installation for
the Fw 190 A-7/R2 and A-8/R2 and the A-9/R8 Sturmflugzeug

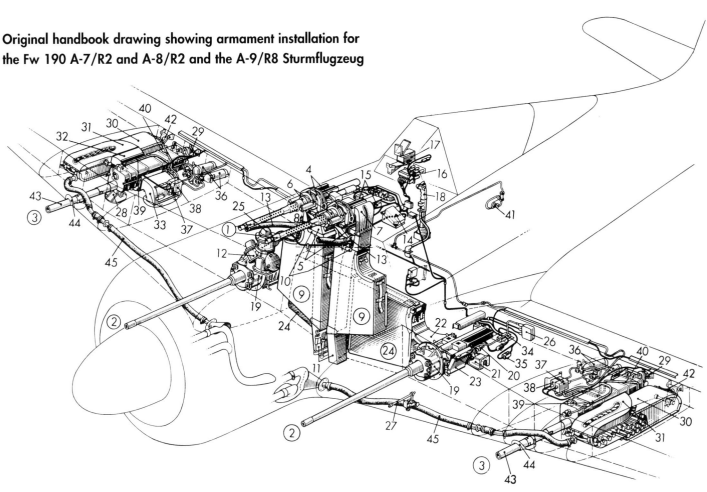

KEY

1. 2 x MG 131 13mm machine guns
2. 2 x MG 151 20mm machine guns
3. 2 x 30mm
4. MG 131 gun mounts
5. Gun mount stand
6. Front shackles
7. Ammunition guides from box
8. Cartridge case and belt connection chutes
9. 13mm ammunition boxes
10. Connectors to ammunition box
11. Spent cartridge case chute
12. MG 131 synchronising equipment
13. MG 131 cooling ducts
14. Electric distributor
15. MG 131 reload controls
16. Gun control and ammunition indicator
17. REVI 16 B gunsight
18. KG 13 B control grip and trigger buttons
19. MG 151 front shackles
20. Rear shackles
21. Rear shackle supports
22. Ammunition guides from box

23. Spent cartridge case chute
24. MG 151 ammunition boxes
25. MG 151 synchronising equipment
26. MG 151 reload controls
27. Armament adjustment gauge socket
28. MK 108 front shackle
29. Ammunition guides from box
30. Mk 108 ammunition box
31. Ammunition guides from box
32. Ammunition feed connector
33. Spent cartridge case chute
34. MK 108 reload controls
35. MK 108 firing convertor
36. Compressed air tanks and reducing valves
37. Electro-pneumatic reload valves
38. Electro-pneumatic trigger valve
39. Compressed air pipe to cocking mechanism
40. Compressed air pipe to trigger mechanism
41. External compressed air filling valve
42. Rear support for MK 108 ammunition box
43. MK 108 barrel
44. Cannon fairing in wing leading edge
45. Ammunition box heating duct

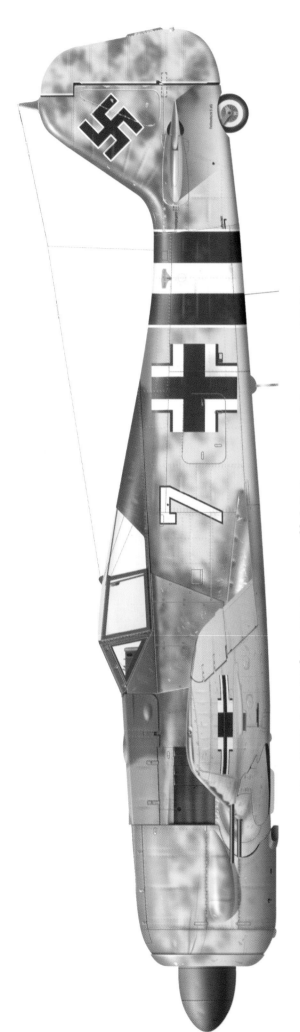

Fw 190 A-6 'White 7' Sturmstaffel 1 Dortmund January 1944

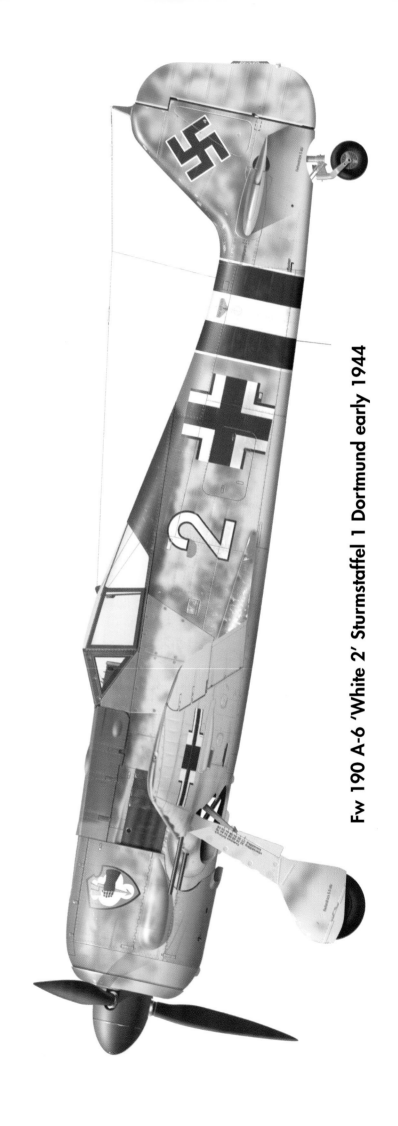

Fw 190 A-6 'White 2' Sturmstaffel 1 Dortmund early 1944

Fw 190 A-7 'White 12' Sturmstaffel 1 Salzwedel April 1944

Standard BMW 801 D

Standard fighter Fw 190 A-7

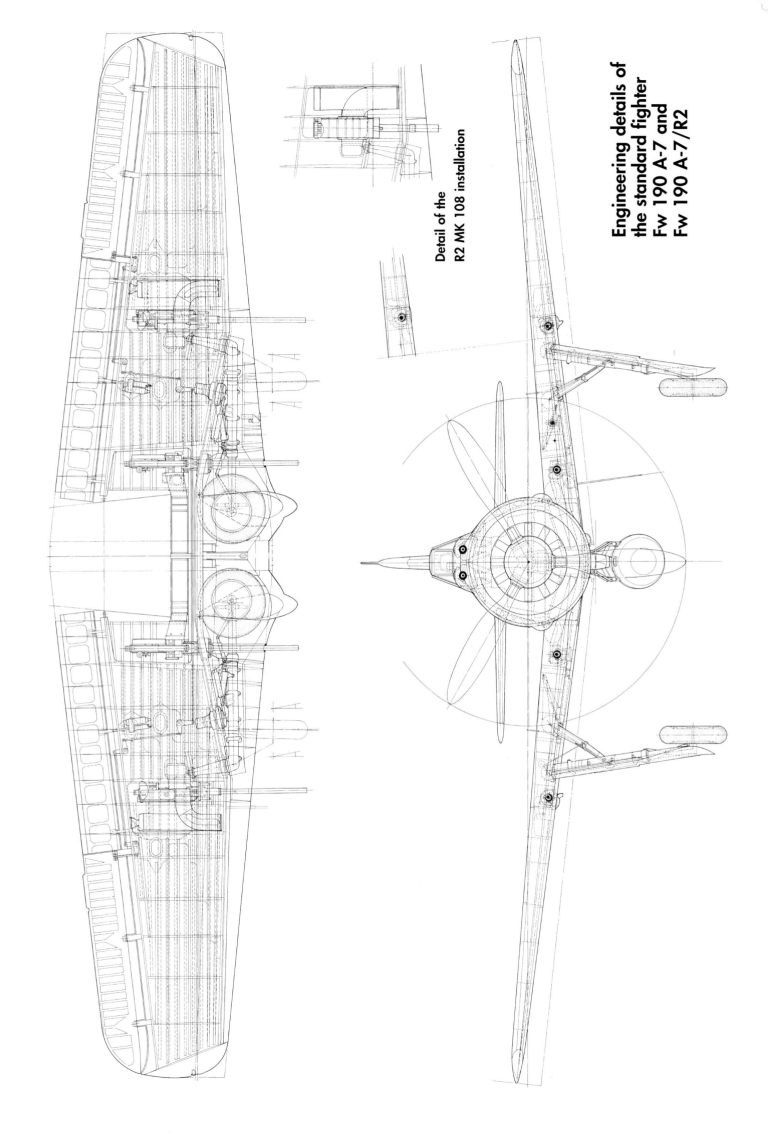

Detail of the
R2 MK 108 installation

**Engineering details of
the standard fighter
Fw 190 A-7 and
Fw 190 A-7/R2**

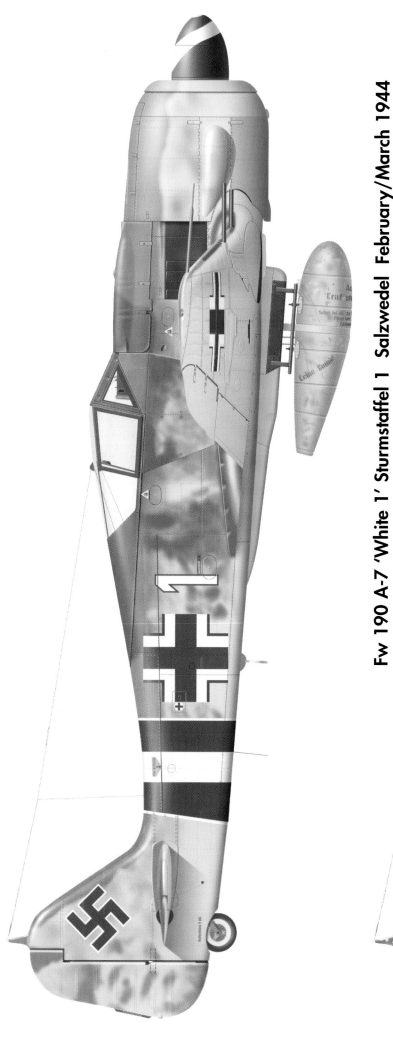

Fw 190 A-7 'White 1' Sturmstaffel 1 Salzwedel February/March 1944

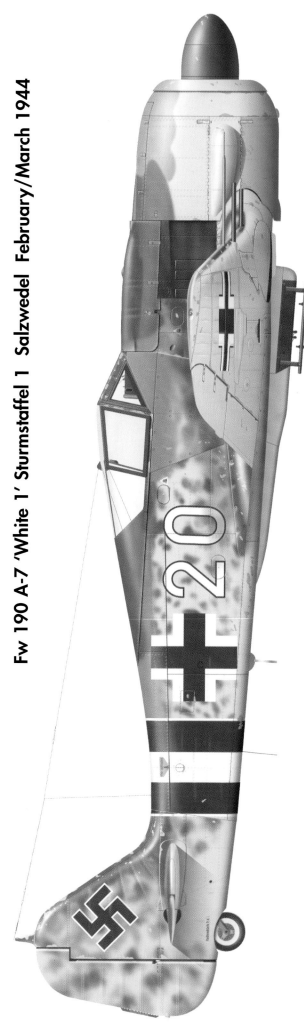

Fw 190 A-7 W.Nr. 642962 'White 20' Sturmstaffel 1 Dortmund/Salzwedel early 1944

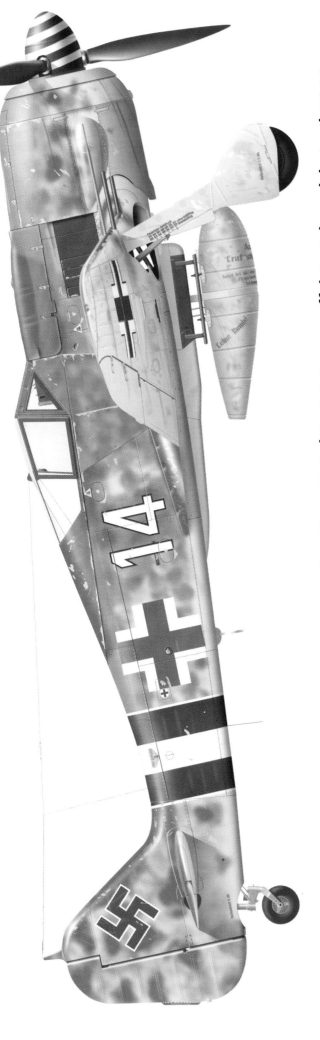

Fw 190 A-7 'White 14' Sturmstaffel 1 Salzwedel April 1944

Notes on Camouflage

All aircraft identified as belonging to Sturmstaffel 1 were painted in the standard factory finish of the time, RLM 74 Graugrün (grey-green), RLM 75 Grauviolett (grey-violet) and RLM 76 Lichtblau (light blue). The most interesting variation in camouflage appears with the addition of fuselage armour. On many of the Sturmstaffel's aircraft, the armour was clearly painted prior to fitting since the demarcation lines do not line up and on some machines, the upper camouflage colour on the armour plate does not match the scheme on the fuselage. The armour was probably finished in RLM 76, with 74 or 75 applied along the top 1/3 and then fitted. However, on some aircraft the armoured panels appear darker than the fuselage 76. In some cases, this may simply be a panel with RLM Grau (grey) 02 primer with only 74/75 applied along the top. Another explanation is a panel with either 02 primer or left in natural metal to which a light coat of 76 was applied, so producing a darker effect than the fuselage 76 which was factory applied and thus had a thicker coat. Notwithstanding this, each aircraft was quite unique due to the field installation of these panels. The 'blinker' armour on the canopies appears to have been RLM 66 Schwarze-Grau (black-grey) or possibly a very dark 74, though this is highly unlikely.

Uffz. Heinz Grosskreuz, "...an extremely good pilot, incredibly gifted."

Below *The USAAF raid on Berlin on 4 March 1944 proved a tough assignment for the pilots of Sturmstaffel 1; Uffz. Gerhard Vivroux (left) shot down a B-17, Fw. Hermann Wahlfeld (second from left) claimed two B-17s destroyed and Fw. Walter Peinemann (far right) was shot down and wounded. The unit also suffered a further Fw 190 damaged. Second from right in this picture is Gefr. Rudolf Pancherz.*

Below right *Taken at the same time as the photograph on the previous page, Vivroux, Wahlfeld and Peinemann are joined by Major Erwin Bacsila who is clad in a USAAF flying jacket. Such items were considered to be prized possesions and 'trophies of war' by Luftwaffe fighter pilots.*

having spotted the fact that his wingman could fly as well as he could. This competitiveness would result in tragedy. The story as I was told it by other pilots was that on 1 March 1944, Gerth and Grosskreuz were "playing" again. Slowly but surely, Grosskreuz overtook his leader. Simultaneously, the two aircraft got closer to each other and Gerth's propeller damaged Grosskreuz's rudder. Unfortunately, Grosskreuz lost control of his aircraft and crashed. Gerth managed to maintain control and landed safely. Of course, it was a shock for us all, but principally for me and Gerth."

"One day, *Uffz.* Hermann Wahlfeld told me and a small group of mechanics why he had volunteered for *Sturmstaffel* 1; he was love-sick. He said that he could not imagine life without his girlfriend. One evening, we were all together chatting and joking when he suddenly said: '*If I do not return tomorrow, you can have "this", you can have "that", and you can have "this" and so on*'. Of course, the following day, all this was forgotten. The most important thing was that Wahlfeld came back alive."

Saturday, 4 March 1944

The Eighth Air Force sent 502 B-17s from the 1st and 3rd Bomb Divisions to attack industrial suburbs in Berlin – the second attempt in two days. With a population of just over 4,300,000 in 1939, the German capital was the greatest commercial and industrial centre on the continent of Europe. Berlin was the "hub" of Nazi Germany's war effort, housing the administrative and ministerial headquarters of all three armed services and it was a major rail centre with twelve main lines meeting there from various directions.

Luckily for the city however, adverse weather conditions prevented all but the 30 aircraft from one combat wing of the 3rd Bomb Division from reaching their primary target and unloading 68 tons of bombs, but inflicting little damage. Of this force, five aircraft were shot down.

Sturmstaffel 1 had taken off from Salzwedel at 12.30 hrs on a southerly course. Having searched the skies for an hour, the unit wheeled to the north and intercepted the Americans near Neuruppin. Closing in from behind and ignoring the murderous defensive fire from the bombers, the *Sturmstaffel* opened fire with their deadly MK 108s at just a few metres from their targets. The result was devastating. *Fw.* Hermann Wahlfeld shot down two bombers, flying through his victims' debris and *Uffz.* Gerhard Vivroux also shot down a B-17.

However, *Fw.* Walter Peinemann was shot down and wounded between Neuruppin and Salzwedel and a further Fw 190 was damaged.

By late 1943, standard USAAF bombing formations deployed over northern Europe were usually made up of a 36-aircraft "combat box". This formation, composed of squadrons of six aircraft broken into two elements of three aircraft, had developed to a great extent from attempts to concentrate as many aircraft together to take advantage of the relatively few radar Pathfinders available at that time. All aircraft in an element flew at the same level, but the elements themselves were separated in

By late 1943, standard USAAF bombing formations deployed over northern Europe were usually made up of a 36-aircraft 'combat box'. This formation was formed of squadrons of six aircraft broken into two elements of three aircraft. All aircraft in an element flew at the same level, but the elements themselves were separated in altitude with a little stagger, forming into high, low and "low-low" positions.

altitude with a little stagger, forming into high, low and "low-low" positions.

These combat boxes then formed a bomber column, with groups in trail, each flying at the same altitude and separated by some 4 miles (6.5 km). Such a formation was much more suitable for 'blind' bombing and also easier for fighters to escort since it was a more 'disciplined' formation than had been used before. However, as with all large formations, it was difficult to hold.

However, by the winter of 1943-1944, combat attrition caused by German fighters attacking *en masse*, plus damage and repair often combined to compel the Eighth Air Force to despatch combat boxes reduced from 36 to just 18 or 21 aircraft.

By March 1944, a typical 21 aircraft box comprised three squadrons, each of two elements; the lead squadron with six aircraft, the low squadron with six and the high squadron with nine. The high and low squadrons flew on opposite sides of the

Left *Two Fw 190 A-7s – 'White 11' and 'White 16' wait on the apron at Saltzwedel early 1944. This photograph shows clearly the fuselage identification markings of Sturmstaffel 1.*

Below *Fifteen Fw 190s of Sturmstaffel 1 – most of them probably A-7s – parked outside the hangar at Salzwedel late February/early March 1944. Nearly all of the aircraft carry drop tanks and it is more than likely that all of them have the black-white-black fuselage identification bands of the Sturmstaffel. Identifiable in the nearest row from left to right are 'White 20' (von Kornatzki's aircraft), 'White 9', 'White 8', 'White 5' and 'White 14'*

Incredulity across the faces of Eighth Air Force bomber crewmen at the briefing room at Polebrook air base in England in the early hours of 6 March 1944. The target was Berlin.

lead, forming a 'V' pointing in the direction of flight and tilted to 45 degrees. The spacing of individual bombers in a box – usually 100-200 ft (30.5-61 m), the equivalent of between one and two wingspans – maximised collective firepower but minimised the risks of unwieldiness, interference with bomb runs and buffeting and displacement from slipstream.

When fully assembled, a bomber stream could stretch for 90 miles (145 km), presenting a problem for the escort fighters which had to zigzag to compensate for the bombers lower speeds. Furthermore, individual fighter groups were not able to stay with the bombers for much more than 30 minutes before fuel ran low, which meant that only a small number of fighters covered the bombers at any one time. It was normal that a third of the escort flew 'up front' to cover the head of the bomber stream and protect it from a German head-on attack.

Monday, 6 March 1944

The Americans tried to reach Berlin again and this time they succeeded.

The Eighth Air Force despatched 504 B-17s and 226 B-24s to strike at industrial targets around the city, escorted and supported by a record 801 USAAF fighters drawn from 17 groups. However, heavy cloud meant that 474 B-17s and 198 B-24s bombed their secondary targets and targets of opportunity in the city itself during breaks in the clouds.

The *Luftwaffe* had been expecting the raid and had prepared itself by practising, several days before, the assembly of large formations of fighters – so-called *Gefechtsverbände* – over the Steinhuder lake north-west of Hannover in an attempt to meet mass with mass. So it was that on this day, no fewer than 19 *Jagdgruppen*, three *Zerstörergruppen* and four *Nachtjagdgruppen*, together with a handful of miscellaneous units, were available to take on the *Viermots*.

Shortly after 11.30 hrs, seven Fw 190s from *Sturmstaffel* 1 joined the Bf 109s of IV./JG 3 as they took off from Salzwedel and headed towards Magdeburg where they were due to form up into a *Gefechtsverband* comprising units drawn from the 1. and 7. *Jagddivisionen* and placed under the command of *Major* Hans Kogler, *Kommandeur* of III./ZG 26. Rendezvous was made at 8,000 m (26,246 ft) near Magdeburg.

Once assembled, this large *Luftwaffe Gefechtsverband* comprised a lead element of 41 Bf 110 and Me 410 *Zerstörer* from II. and III./ZG 26 and I. and II./ZG 76, many equipped with underwing batteries of four 21 cm WGr. mortars intended to

B-17s of the 303rd Bomb Group ride the Flak on their way to Berlin, 6 March 1944.

break up the approaching enemy formation. Behind the *Zerstörer* came a force of 72 Bf 109s and Fw 190s from I., II. and IV./JG 3, *Sturmstaffel* 1, JG 302 and the *Jasta* Erla works defence flight.

Towards 12.30 hrs, the enemy bombers were sighted – 112 B-17 Flying Fortresses of the 1st and 94th Combat Wings of the 1st Bomb Division, formed from the 91st, 351st, 401st and 457th Bomb Groups. The twin-engine heavy fighters went in first and fired off their mortars. As they did so, P-51 Mustangs of Lt. Col. Don Blakeslee's 4th Fighter Group dived out of the sun to intercept and in doing so forced the *Zerstörer* pilots to break off their attacks early. The result was that many of the mortars exploded way off target.

Following behind the Bf 110s and Me 410s, the Bf 109s of IV./JG 3 attacked the bombers head on and from out of the sun. By the time the action was over, the *Gruppe* would claim 12 of the bombers either shot down or struck out of formation as well as one P-51.

For *Sturmstaffel* 1, it was to be the most successful day since the unit's formation. Moving in to attack from the

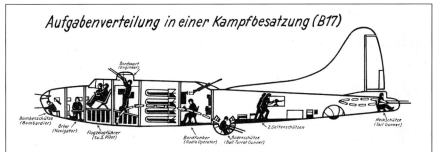

Aufgabenverteilung in einer Kampfbesatzung (B17)

3. Die einzelnen Besatzungsmitglieder haben folgende Aufgaben:

Der erste Flugzeugführer (First Pilot)fliegt im Verbandsflug nach den Flugbewegungen seines Führerflugzeuges, im Einzel- flug steuert er nach den Anweisungen des Orters.
Der zweite Flugzeugführer (Second oder Co-Pilot) unterstützt den ersten Flugzeugführer bei Start und Landung des Flugzeu- ges und den Orter bei der Navigation.
Der Orter (Navigator) ist verantwortlich für die gesamte Na- vigation, bedient die Navigationsgeräte (auch das Hyperbel- gerät) und führt das Logbuch.
Im Gegensatz zu brit. Ortern ist er jedoch nur in dem Ver- bandsführerflugzeug voll ausgelastet, dem die übrigen Flug- zeuge nur nachzufliegen haben.
Bei Feindberührung bedient der Orter das rechte MG. in der Kanzel.
Der Bombenschütze (Bombardier) unterstützt den Orter bei der Sichtnavigation, beobachtet den Luftraum nach vorn und weist beim Zielanflug und Bombenwurf den Flugzeugführer ein. Bei Feindberührung bedient er das linke MG. in der Kanzel.

Beide Flugzeugführer, der Orter und der Bombenschütze, sind im allgemeinen Offiziere, in letzter Zeit sind jedoch auch Mannschaftsdienstgrade aufgetreten.
Der Funker (Radio Operator) bedient die Funkgeräte und das obere Einzel-MG. im Rumpf.
Der Bordwart (Engineer) überwacht die technischen Einrich- tungen an Bord (Behälterschaltung usw.) und wird im allge- meinen als Bordschütze im oberen Turm (upper turret) einge- setzt.
Ein Bordschütze (Gunner) bedient den Turm (Ball turret) an der Rumpfunterseite.
2 Bordschützen werden als Seitenschützen für die MG's im hinteren Rumpf verwendet.
Von diesen 3 Bordschützen sind 2 in geringem Umfang als Hilfsbordwarte und Hilfsbordfunker (assistant engineer bzw. radio operator) ausgebildet.
Ein besonders guter Bordschütze ist als Heckschütze (tail gunner) eingeteilt.

Above *A page taken from a German training manual showing the crew positions on board an American B-17 Flying Fortress. Such information was invaluable to Luftwaffe fighter pilots who devised optimum tactics with which to bring down heavy bombers at minimum risk. Knowledge of the location of the gun positions was especially vital.*

Below *A similiar plan of a B-17 showing gun and fuel tank positions together with tank capacities. The wing- mounted fuel tanks formed prime target areas for German fighter pilots.*

Below *This formation of B-17s appears to have lost its tactical cohesion and may well be returning from a mission with depleted ranks.*

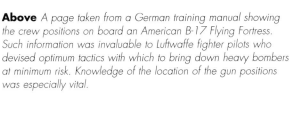

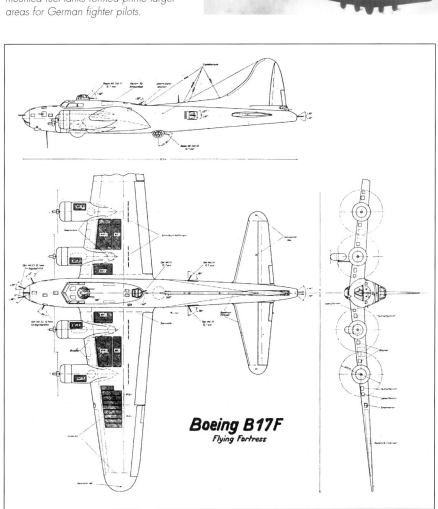

Boeing B17F
Flying Fortress

Mechanics work on the Fw 190s of
Sturmstaffel 1 outside the hangars at
Salzwedel, late February/March 1944. These
aircraft are all fitted with 300 ltr drop tanks
and their propeller spinners have been painted
with the later-style white spirals.

Below Oblt. Othmar Zehart is flanked by
Uffz. Kurt Röhrich (left) and Ofw. Gerhard
Marburg (right). Zehart scored his second
victory over a B-17 on 6 March 1944.

Below centre Lt. Gerhard Dost who scored
his first victory over a B-17 during the USAAF
attack on Berlin on 6 March 1944 only to be
shot down by Mustangs shortly afterwards.

Below right Uffz. Kurt Röhrich, an Austrian
pilot, was killed in action on 19 July 1944,
with 12 claims.

rear, the *Staffel* closed in on B-17s of the 91st Bomb Group. *Uffz.* Kurt Röhrich scored
his third victory at 12.35 hrs, together with *Uffz.* Willi Maximowitz who claimed a
Herausschuss and *Lt.* Gerhard Dost who registered his first victory. Three minutes later,
Fw. Hermann Wahlfeld who had shot down a bomber just two days before, added to
his personal score and recorded his third victory. *Oblt.* Othmar Zehart followed at
12.55 hrs when he scored his second victory.

One *Sturmstaffel* 1 Fw 190 collided with '*My Darling Also*', a B-17G (42-31578)
of the 91st Bomb Group piloted by 1st Lt. B. Tibbetts. The Focke-Wulf descended
slightly as it approached and took hits, but then climbed "relentlessly" towards '*My
Darling Also*' – by now already badly damaged by fire from the German fighter – until
it hit the Boeing knocking away the entire right stabiliser. The B-17 began to fall out of
control. Eight crew were killed and two bailed out and were taken prisoner.

One Fw 190 from *Sturmstaffel* 1 returned to Salzwedel with 60% damage,
effectively a write-off. In a post mission report, the 1st Bomb Division described the
attack on the 1st and 94th Combat Wings as "vicious".

Following his victory, *Lt.* Gerhard Dost was killed in his Fw 190 A-7 'White 20'
while attempting to escape two P-51s near Salzwedel.

In what may have been a second mission intended to attack the bombers on their
return run, *Lt.* Werner Gerth claimed his second and third victories at 14.05 hrs and
14.08 hrs respectively.

In all, by the time the *Gefechts-verband* broke off its attack, having expended
both fuel and ammunition, eight B-17s had been shot down and three more destroyed
in collisions. Four P-51 escort fighters also went down in the Berlin area. However, for
the Germans, the price of this 'success' was high; of the seven Bf 110s of III./ZG 26

which went into action, five were destroyed and the remaining two damaged. Eleven further *Zerstörer* were destroyed and at least two more damaged. For the single engined fighters, losses were five Bf 109s and two Fw 190s.

In total, the *Luftwaffe* suffered 87 single- or twin-engine fighters lost or damaged on 6 March. Thirty six aircrew were killed and another 27 wounded. On the American side, 53 B-17s and 16 B-24s failed to return, 293 B-17s and 54 B-24s were damaged and five B-17s and one B-24 written off. Seventeen crew were killed, 31 wounded and 686 were listed as missing.

But of even greater psychological impact on the Germans was the fact that Berlin could no longer be considered immune from attack, no longer out of range. The pressure on the pilots of the *Sturmstaffel* and the other outnumbered fighter units operating in the defence of the Reich could now only grow.

The certificate confirming the award of the Iron Cross Second Class to Uffz. Gerhard Vivroux of Sturmstaffel 1 on 6 March 1944. The certificate has been signed by Oberst Günther Lützow, the Kommandeur of 1.Jagddivision based at Döberitz. Vivroux was awarded the Iron Cross First Class on 24 April 1944.

Wednesday, 8 March 1944

The Allies were not allowing Berlin any respite. On 8 March, 320 B-17s and 150 B-24s bombed the VKF ball-bearing plant at Erkner. Others bombed targets of opportunity in the German capital. As an indication of the dramatic odds at which the *Luftwaffe* defence now fought, a record 891 USAAF fighters provided escort and

Fw 190 A-7 W.Nr. 642962 'White 20' pictured probably at Salzwedel and the aircraft in which Lt. Gerhard Dost met his fate on 6 March 1944. This aircraft, which was also flown by Major von Kornatzki, lacks the twin MG 131 nose guns and is seen prior to the application of white spirals to its spinner.

Three views taken from the hangar roof at Salzwedel showing Fw 190s 'White 1' and 'White 2' of Sturmstaffel 1 parked on the apron whilst other aircraft taxi out towards the runway.

support. Eighteen of these were lost and a further 16 written off as a result of the raid.

At Salzwedel, IV./JG 3 was scrambled to intercept at 13.48 hrs, and it is more than likely that the unit took off accompanied by the six operational Fw 190s of *Sturmstaffel* 1. At 7,500 m (24,606 ft) over Magdeburg, the fighters formed up into a *Gefechtsverband* with a small number of Bf 110 *Zerstörer* from ZG 26 and other elements of JG 3.

Following a course to the north-west, at 13.25 hrs, the *Gefechtsverband* sighted the American bombers at 6,000 m (22,310 ft) flying east-south-east with strong fighter escort. Once again, the *Zerstörer* went in first, followed by JG 3 which mounted a frontal attack and once again, the *Gruppe* demonstrated its extraordinary tenacity by claiming 13 victories.

Success for the *Sturmstaffel* however, was restricted to one B-17 brought down by *Lt.* Richard Franz. It was to be Franz's second – but hard-won – victory; his first had been scored whilst he had been with JG 77. He recalls how it was to shoot down a heavy bomber in conditions such as those prevailing on 8 March: "At this time, the *Sturmstaffel* was the only unit in the *Luftwaffe*, which attacked bombers from the rear, flying a 'V' formation. The close 'V' formation provided a very strong attacking force with extreme firepower, so that when we engaged we were always successful. On one hand, unlike the usual head-on tactic, this gave us much more time to attack and shoot, but on the other hand, the Fortress gunners had the same advantage. In my opinion – and as I recall – the defensive bomber formation was very effective, because in trying to attack it, it was very difficult to find even one angle at which you were not subject to defensive fire. In addition, flying at the outer perimeters of the formation, there was often what we called a "Flak cruiser" – aircraft without bombs but carrying additional machine guns and cannon. Another problem was trying to bring our very heavy birds into position before we were caught by the escort fighters, which sometimes happened and brought us severe losses. It was the P-51s and P-47s that caused us the heaviest losses in our *Staffel*. Their control was very good, the tactical direction of their leaders was good and their endurance was much higher than ours in most cases."

Thursday, 9 March 1944

Bad weather brought some relief to Berlin from further bombardment with more than 330 B-17s from the Eighth Air Force forced to execute an "area attack". The 2nd Bombardment Division's 150 B-24 Liberators hit various secondary targets around Braunschweig, Hannover and Nienburg.

One comfort for the Americans was that the *Luftwaffe* fighter force – including *Sturmstaffel* 1 – remained grounded due to the weather.

Thursday, 23 March 1944

Poor weather over most of north-west Europe denied the American air commanders an opportunity to launch further effective incursions for some two weeks. Despite this, attacks were made against targets in southern Germany on the 16th and against aircraft factories and airfields – again in the south – two days later. On both these occasions, the *Luftwaffe* launched scattered but extremely aggressive fighter attacks and USAAF bomber losses were high. On the 22nd, a force of 657 heavies returned to Berlin, the continuing bad weather having diverted them from their original targets of Oranienburg and Basdorf. Twelve bombers were lost and an astonishing 347 damaged.

Then, on the 23rd, a total of 707 B-17s and B-24s headed for the cities of Braunschweig and Münster and the airfields at Achmer (*Sturmstaffel* 1's original base) and Handorf – all secondary targets and targets of opportunity due to bad weather.

Shortly before 10.00 hrs, *Sturmstaffel* 1, together with aircraft from IV./JG 3, took off from Salzwedel and set off for Magdeburg where they assembled at 10.15 hrs with more aircraft from II./JG 3 out of Gardelegen. Once assembled into a composite battle group, this force then made west towards an area south-east of Münster. The significance of this operation is illustrated by the fact that, on this occasion, the *Sturmstaffel* was led by its commander, *Major* von Kornatzki, who, it will be remembered, apparently flew few combat sorties.

At 11.00 hrs, contact was made with the 296 B-17s of the 1st Bombardment Division which were flying due west having bombed their target at Münster and covered by a heavy escort of P-51 Mustangs. The German formation overflew the bomber *Pulk* from the left, wheeled ahead and at 11.20, from north of Hamm, launched a massed frontal attack.

Major Hans-Günter von Kornatzki, commander of Sturmstaffel 1 (second from right) and Major Friedrich-Karl Müller, Gruppenkommandeur of IV./JG 3 hold a discussion with the pilots of Sturmstaffel 1 outside the control building at Salzwedel. Recognisable in this picture are (from far left) Heinz Steffen, Gerhard Vivroux, Friedrich-Karl Müller, Siegfried Müller (back to camera), Werner Gerth, von Kornatzki, and Kurt Röhrich.

Within the space of 10 minutes, *Sturmstaffel* 1 accounted for six B-17s shot down or forced out of formation.

Kornatzki claimed a *Herausschuss* at 11.25 hrs, which represented his fifth overall victory, as did *Lt.* Friedrich Dammann at 11.17 hrs which was his first score. Other bombers were shot down by *Uffz.* Gerhard Vivroux (11.15 hrs), *Uffz.* Kurt Röhrich (11.15) *Flg.* Wolfgang Kosse (11.20 hrs) and by *Uffz.* Willi Maximowitz (11.15) who shot his victim down over his home town.

Will Maximowitz was born in 1920, a native of Wuppertal-Barmen and had joined the *Sturmstaffel* from JG 1. Shortly after shooting down the B-17, Maximowitz's aircraft was hit and he was wounded after taking to his parachute. Oscar Boesch, another *Sturmstaffel* pilot, remembers: "Maximowitz was a wild man and always carried a machine-gun with him. He didn't want to be captured by anyone."

The *Sturmstaffel's* success against the bombers on 23 March, surpassed the efforts of IV./JG 3, which sent four B-17s and one P-51 down. However, the unit's accomplishments were not achieved without cost; *Fw.* Hermann Wahlfeld, who had rammed a bomber in January, went down near Lippstadt and *Fw.* Otto Weissenberger was killed near Nordick (Heiden).

These losses were replaced by the arrival the same day of two experienced *Leutnante,* Rudolf Metz from JG 5 and Siegfried Müller from JG 51.

Müller recalled: "At the end of 1943, I was with II./JG 51 in Nisch, Yugoslavia, when the call came from *Reichsmarschall* Göring for volunteers for a *Sturmstaffel.* In view of my two victories, I believed that I could contribute my experience and so volunteered, in order to play my part in shooting down the American bombers that were causing so much destruction over our Fatherland. On 24 March, I flew my first mission with *Sturmstaffel* 1, holding the stick of Fw 190 'White 17'."

Altogether, the month of March 1944 cost *Sturmstaffel* 1 three pilots killed, two wounded, six Fw 190s destroyed and four assessed at 60% damage.

Throughout November 1943 and early 1944, the Eighth Air Force conducted attacks against a range of targets across central and north-west Germany. Here, Flying Fortresses head for Bremen, Germany's second largest port. The city was bombed three times by the Eighth.

Sturmstaffel 1 Victories – February-March 1944

Date	Pilot	Aircraft	Time
10/02/44	Ofhr. Heinz Steffen	B-17 (1)	11.15
			Rheine area, 7,500m
11/02/44	Flg. Wolfgang Kosse	B-17 (18)	12.35
	Ofhr. Heinz Steffen	B-17 (2)	12.40
21/02/44	Uffz. Kurt Röhrich	B-17 (2)	15.00
	Fw. Gerhard Marburg	B-17 (1)	15.15
	Fw. Gerhard Marburg	B-17 HSS (2)	15.25
22/02/44	Lt. Werner Gerth	B-17 (1)	13.40
04/03/44	Fw. Hermann Wahlfeld	B-17 (2)	13.30
	Uffz. Gerhard Vivroux	B-17 (1)	13.30
06/03/44	Uffz. Kurt Röhrich	B-17 (3)	12.35
	Gefr. Willi Maximowitz	B-17 HSS(2)	12.35
	Lt. Gerhard Dost	B-17 (1)	12.35
	Fw. Hermann Wahlfeld	B-17 (3)	12.38
	Oblt. Othmar Zehart	B-17 (2)	12.55
	Lt. Werner Gerth	B-17 (2)	14.05
	Lt. Werner Gerth	B-17 (3)	14.08
08/03/44	Lt. Richard Franz	B-17 (2)	
23/03/44	Uffz. Willi Maximowitz	B-17 (3)	11.15
	Uffz. Gerhard Vivroux	B-17 (2)	11.15
	Uffz. Kurt Röhrich	B-17 (4)	11.15
	Lt. Friedrich Dammann	B-17 HSS (1)	11.17
	Flg. Wolfgang Kosse	B-17 (19)	11.20
	Maj. Hans-Günter von Komatzki	B-17 HSS (5)	11.25

Sturmstaffel 1 Losses – February-March 1944

21/02/44	Uffz. Erich Lambertus (KIA)	Fw 190 A-7 (642559) White 3	100% in combat 25 km north of Lübecke
21/02/44	Uffz. Walter Köst (KIA)	Fw 190 A-7 (642975)	100% in combat Sundern near Lübecke
01/03/44	Uffz. Heinz Grosskreuz (KIA)	Fw 190 A-6 (551108) White 14	100% Ferry flight crashed near Uelzen
04/03/44		Fw 190 A- in combat	? %
04/03/44	Fw. Werner Peinemann (WIA)	Fw 190 A-7 (340028) White 8	100% in combat near Bad Wilsnack
06/03/44		Fw 190 A-	? % in combat
06/03/44	Lt. Gerhard Dost (KIA)	Fw 190 A-7 (642962) White 20	100% in combat near Salzwedel
23/03/44		Fw 190 A-	100% in combat
23/03/44		Fw 190 A-	? % in combat
23/03/44	Uffz. Willi Maximowitz (WIA)	Fw 190 A-6 (551099) White 10	100% in combat near Wuppertal-Barmen (Hamm/Westf.)
23/03/44	Fw. Hermann Wahlfeld (KIA)	Fw 190 A-6 (470208) White 9	100% in combat near Lippstadt
23/03/44	Fw. Otto Weissenberger (KIA)	Fw 190 A-6 (531057) White 9	100% in combat near Nordick (Berbern)

Above *The resilience of the armoured Panzerglas canopy side panels can be seen in this picture of Uffz. Willi Maximowitz's Fw 190 A-6 'White 10' which took at least two hits from enemy fire. Indication of damage can also be seen just above the white aircraft code numeral on the fuselage side. Maximowitz shot down a B-17 over Wuppertal on 23 March 1944.*

Below *Further testimony to the level of protection offered to pilots from the installation of armoured Panzerglas canopy side panels can be seen in this photograph of Fw. Hermann Walhfeld sitting in the cockpit of his Fw 190 following an encounter with USAAF P-51 Mustangs. The panel received a direct hit but Wahlfeld escaped unharmed. Unfortunately, his luck did not hold on 23 March 1944, when he was shot down near Lippstadt in his Fw 190 A-6 'White 9'.*

Above *Uffz. Gerhard Vivroux stands before his Fw 190 A-7. Note the black-white-black fuselage identification band and the armoured glass panels on the canopy. Vivroux claimed a B-17 on 23 March 1944.*

Lt. Siegfried Müller joined Sturmstaffel 1 from II./JG 51 and flew his first mission with his new unit on 24 March 1944.

Above 23 March 1944: Flg. Wolfgang Kosse (second from right) describes his victory over a B-17 north of Hamm to Major Erwin Bacsila (right). To the left of Kosse is Uffz. Kurt Röhrich who also claimed a B-17 during the mission. Listening to Kosse third from left, is Lt. Rudolf Metz, a newly arrived pilot with the Sturmstaffel who had come from JG 5, whilst second from left can be seen the unit's "Spiess".

Below Same place, same time. Note the drop tank lying on the ground in front of the Fw 190 in the background.

A reference report on Leutnant Rudolf Metz prepared by his former unit, IV./JG 5, on 28 March 1944, in readiness for his transfer to Sturmstaffel 1 at Salzwedel. The report advises that Metz, who had served as Technical Officer, had been awarded the Iron Cross 2nd Class and the Front Flug Spange for Fighters in Bronze and Silver. He is described as a fearless, determined fighter pilot with initiative and a positive attitude towards his work.

5. FIERCE ONSLAUGHT

Saturday, 8 April 1944

On 8 April 1944, *Herr* Lehmkuhl, a Focke-Wulf technician, reported that the fitting of protective external armour plating to 18 Fw 190s of *Sturmstaffel* 1 had been completed without problems. The aircraft so fitted were:

W.Nr.

431003 Fw 190 A-7 sub-type built by Ago at Oschersleben. A total of 15.47 hrs flying time over 16 flights.

642969 Fw 190 A-7 sub-type built by Fieseler at Kassel. A total of 5.09 hrs flying time over 7 flights.

340286 Fw 190 A-7 sub-type built by Focke-Wulf, probably at Bremen. A total of 8.57 hrs flying time over 18 flights.

340030 Fw 190 A-7 sub-type built by Focke-Wulf, probably at Bremen. This aircraft, coded 'White 4', was lost in combat on 8 April 1944, at Fallensleben, piloted by *Lt*. Dammann of *Sturmstaffel* 1. A total of 16.28 hrs flying time over 18 flights.

643937 Fw 190 A-7 sub-type built by Fieseler at Kassel. This aircraft, coded 'White 5' was lost in combat on 8 April 1944, near Uelzen, piloted by *Uffz*. Kukuk of *Sturmstaffel* 1. A total of 8.02 hrs flying time 5 over flights.

550876 Fw 190 A-6 sub-type built by Ago at Oschersleben. A total of 18.55 hrs flying time over 39 flights.

431162 Fw 190 A-7 sub-type built by Ago at Oschersleben. A total of 4.22 hrs flying time over 6 flights.

431176 Fw 190 A-7 sub-type built by Ago at Oschersleben. A total of 3.23 hrs flying time over 7 flights.

340306 Fw 190 A-7 sub-type built by Focke-Wulf, probably at Bremen. A total of 4.12 hrs flying time over 6 flights.

431172 Fw 190 A-? sub-type built by Ago at Oschersleben. A total of 12.49 hrs flying time over 21 flights. As an aircraft of 14.(*Sturm*)/JG 3, it was lost in combat on 15 August 1944, near Liège, piloted by *Uffz*. Wolfgang Engel, the sub-type given as an A-8, but probably an A-7.

642974 Fw 190 A-7 sub-type built by Fieseler at Kassel. A total of 7.06 hrs flying time over 7 flights. Of note is the fact that W.Nr. 642975, W.Nr. 642974's sister aircraft, was an aircraft of *Sturmstaffel* 1 lost in combat on 21 February 1944, near Lübeck, piloted by *Uffz*. Köst, coded 'White 19'.

531073 Fw 190 A-6 sub-type built by Fieseler at Kassel. A total of 22.17 hrs flying time over 39 flights.

431181 Fw 190 A-7 sub-type built by Ago at Oschersleben. A total of 5.22 hrs flying time over 8 flights. This aircraft was lost in combat on 14 April 1944, near Ebersbach/Neckar, piloted by *Uffz*. Fink, of *Sturmstaffel* 1 and coded 'White 14'.

340340 Fw 190 A-7 sub-type built by Focke-Wulf, probably at Bremen. A total of 14.51 hrs flying time over 21 flights. Some records report this aircraft was lost in combat on 4 April 1944, near Fallensleben, piloted by *Uffz*. Rohde of *Sturmstaffel* 1 and coded 'White 15'.

340264 Fw 190 A-7 sub-type built by Focke-Wulf, probably at Bremen. A total of 19.43 hrs flying time over 28 flights.

470786 Fw 190 A-6 sub-type built by Arado at Warnemünde. A total of 5.23 hrs flying time over 7 flights. It was later an aircraft of 11.(*Sturm*)/JG 3 and was lost in combat on 19 May 1944, near Oldenburg, piloted by *Uffz*. Friedrich Schnaars.

470085 Fw 190 A-6 sub-type built by Arado at Warnemünde. A total of 42.22 hrs
        flying time over 50 flights.
643934 Fw 190 A-7/R2 sub-type built by Fieseler at Kassel. A total of 5.46 hrs
        flying time over 4 flights.

April 1944 saw the end of the Combined Bomber Offensive and the US Eighth Air Force, together with the other strategic forces, passed to General Dwight D. Eisenhower, the newly appointed Supreme Allied Commander. Still the weather continued to hamper American heavy bomber operations however, and during the first week of the month only the 2nd and 3rd Bombardment Divisions were able to mount operations in unsettled weather against targets in France.

"All movements in the battlefield have but one end in view, the development of fire in greater volume and more effectively than that of the opposing force."
Thomas Miller Maguire (1849-1920), The Development of Tactics, 1904

Even on the 8th, fog prevented a large part of the 1st Bombardment Division from taking off to attack its assigned airfield target at Oldenburg. The 3rd Bombardment Division despatched 255 B-17s to airfields across north-west Germany and the B-24 Liberators of the 2nd Bombardment Division headed for aircraft production plants at Braunschweig as well as Langenhagen airfield and other targets in the Rosslingen area. The whole force was protected by 780 fighters.

Once again accompanying IV./JG 3, *Sturmstaffel* 1 took from Salzwedel at 13.05 hrs and formed up into a *Gefechtsverband* with *Stab*, I. and II./JG 3. One hour later the *Gefechtsverband* began its approach against a large incoming formation of B-17s and B-24s with fighter escort, north west of Braunschweig. Launching a massed frontal attack over Fallersleben, a massive air battle commenced, the sky swirling with P-51s, P-38s, Bf 109s and Fw 190s as the bombers lumbered on into their bomb run.

The *Sturmstaffel* attacked a box of Liberators and within a matter of minutes had shot down four of them; *Uffz.* Kurt Röhrich – his fifth victory at 14.20 hrs, *Lt.* Siegfried Müller – his third victory at 14.20 hrs, *Uffz.* Heinz Steffen – a *Herausschuss* representing his third claim at 14.20 hrs and *Lt.* Richard Franz – his third victory.

Inset *Not far from where the picture below was taken, Major Erwin Bacsila smiles for a photograph with Lt. Rudolf Metz to his left.*

Below *The engines of six Fw 190s of Sturmstaffel 1 running up on the apron outside the hangar at Salzwedel, March/April 1944.*

Lt. Richard Franz remembers: "After this mission, I had the opportunity to meet a crew member of the bomber I had shot down. I landed at Magdeburg airfield and met him there in the operations room. He was a lieutenant, his name was Andy and he was the only member of the crew who had survived the attack. We had a good talk and he presented me with his flying jacket – half leather and half silk with 24 previous missions written in ink on the silk part of the jacket, including the date and target. He told me that this was their last mission and that had they returned they would have been posted back to the States. But he also felt lucky to be alive. I had that jacket until the end of the war, when I was shot down for the last time on 25 April 1945 by a Russian fighter over Berlin."

The *Staffel* suffered three pilots killed; *Lt.* Friedrich Dammann and *Uffz.* Karl Rhode went down over Fallersleben, whilst *Uffz.* Walter Kukuk was shot down over Uelzen. *Lt.* Siegfried Müller made a belly landing near Salzwedel.

Sunday, 9 April 1944

The USAAF targeted aircraft plants and airfields in north east Germany – Rahmel, Marienburg, Tutow, Parchim, Posen, Warnemünde and Rostock-Marienehe. Over 400 heavies were effective over the range of targets, escorted by 719 fighters, most of them P-47s.

An unknown number of aircraft from *Sturmstaffel* 1 took off with IV./JG 3 at 10.35 hrs. A *Gefechtsverband* was assembled over the Baltic coast near Rügen where an air battle broke out between the German fighters, the bombers and their P-51 escorts shortly before midday.

A second force from IV./JG 3 took off from Salzwedel twenty minutes after the first.

The *Sturmstaffel* achieved only one victory, when *Flg.* Wolfgang Kosse shot down a B-24, claiming his twentieth victory. The second force returned without any success.

One Fw 190 was destroyed on the ground at Salzwedel.

An "Easter Present" for the Führer: USAAF armourers prepare to load a bomb into a B-17 prior to the large-scale raid on 9 April 1944.

Tuesday, 11 April 1944

The Americans launched an all-out assault against centres of aircraft production in eastern Germany. A record-breaking force of 917 B-17s and B-24s was assembled to strike at the Focke-Wulf plants at Posen (Poznan) and Sorau, the Junkers plants at Bernburg and Halberstadt, the Pommerische Motorenbau works at Stettin and Cottbus and various assembly plants at Oschersleben. This enormous armada was protected by more than 800 fighters drawn from 13 fighter groups from the Eighth Air Force and four from the Ninth Air Force's Third Division, though with bomber resources stretched over such a wide range of deep penetration targets, even this escort was only just adequate and weather conditions had improved only marginally over those prevailing on the 9th.

Some USAAF fighters had arrived over Holland and Northern Germany as early as 09.10 hrs, but did not succeed in disturbing the co-ordination and assembly of German defence units. Instead, they set about strafing airfields and attacked 25 trains, destroying 21 locomotives before returning across the Channel.

The first – northern – element of the bomber force approached the Dutch coast at 09.09 hrs, 90 km (56 mls) north west of Vlieland, crossing the coast between Westerland and Rendsburg and proceeded via Laaland and Rügen into Pomerania, Stargard, Poznan and Stettin and also via the island of Fehmarn towards Rostock.

The second – southern – element crossed the Dutch coast between Bergen op Zoom and Den Haag from 09.55 hrs onwards. The formation headed east across the Zuider Zee following the lines Kloppenburg-Osnabrück, Soltau-Hildesheim, Stendal-Dessau to attack Oschersleben and Bernburg.

In response, the I. *Jagdkorps* sent up a total of 432 single- and twin-engined fighters drawn from 1., 2. and 3. *Jagddivisionen*. According to the Eighth Air Force, the *Luftwaffe* performed "... *one of its most severe and well co-ordinated defences marked by skilful handling of a considerable number of twin-engined day fighters in the Stettin area and single-engine fighters in the Hannover-Oschersleben area.*"

Both sides were tested.

At 10.05 hrs, *Sturmstaffel* 1 and IV./JG 3 received the *Alarmstart* and took off from Salzwedel to form up into a *Gefechtsverband* with elements of various units drawn from 1. and 3. *Jagddivisionen*. The Americans were sighted some forty minutes later between Braunschweig and Halberstadt. *Sturmstaffel* 1 separated from IV./JG 3, with the latter unit directing its attack against a combat box of B-17s, whilst the *Sturmstaffel* closed in on a formation of some 50 B-24 Liberators from the 2nd Bombardment Division in the Hildesheim area. For the Americans it was to be carnage, whilst the *Sturmstaffel* enjoyed the most successful action in its short-lived history. Five B-24s were either shot down or cut away from their formation in 60 seconds thanks to the efforts of *Lt.* Rudolf Metz (2nd victory), *Lt.* Werner Gerth (4th victory), *Ofw.* Gerhard Marburg (3rd victory), *Uffz.* Kurt Röhrich (6th victory, a *Herausschuss*) and *Lt.* Siegfried Müller (4th victory).

More followed; two minutes later, Gerhard Marburg went on to claim a *Herausschuss*, whilst Werner Gerth shot down another B-24 at 11.18 hrs. Kurt Röhrich accounted for one of the P-47 escorts, the first fighter to be shot down by the *Sturmstaffel*.

In its Narrative of Operations, the Eighth Air Force reported on the combined *Sturmstaffel* 1 and JG 3 attack: "... *the leading group on Oschersleben was not attacked until it reached the IP near Hildesheim where about 50 Fw 190s and Me 109s were seen. A number of enemy aircraft passed through the formation in ones and twos from 10 o'clock making unpressed attacks. The last combat wing on Oschersleben encountered about 25 Fw 190s and Me 109s which attacked aggressively just after the target. Enemy aircraft would come in three or four abreast or in a V formation from ahead or high and level.*"

Curiously, this narrative makes no mention of any German attacks mounted from the rear and it may have been that, on this occasion, the *Sturmstaffel* attacked from the front in mass formation with the other units involved.

Following this action, a few *Sturmjäger* together with elements of IV./JG 3 joined up and flew in formation back to Salzwedel. Once landed, they quickly refuelled and rearmed for a second mission directed against the returning bombers. They took off at

On Thursday, 11 April 1944, five B-24s were either shot down or cut away from their formation by Sturmstaffel 1 in 60 seconds over Hildesheim. One of the victorious pilots was Lt. Rudolf Metz, formerly of JG 5.

Lt. Siegfried Müller scored his fourth victory with Sturmstaffel 1 on 11 April 1944. His victim was a B-24 Liberator. Note the Deutsches Kreuz which he received during the last days of the war.

Uffz. Gerhard Vivroux leaves the cockpit of Fw 190 'White 3' following his return from another mission. On 11 April 1944, he accounted for a B-17 shot down, his third victory.

Fw 190 A-7s 'White 12' and 'White 14' undergoing maintenance at Salzwedel, April 1944. Having scored his first victory on 13 April 1944, Uffz. Heinrich Fink of Sturmstaffel 1 was killed the following day near Ebersbach in the latter aircraft. A Bf 109 G-6 of I./JG 3 can be seen in the background.

12.40 hrs. Heading to the north-west, it took them only 15 minutes to seek prey. Thirty minutes later, having assembled into attack position, they closed in on a formation of B-17s, most probably from the 3rd Bombardment Division returning from bombing Rostock and Stettin. *Uffz.* Gerhard Vivroux of *Sturmstaffel* 1 shot down a B-17 (his third victory) at 13.18 hrs, whilst pilots of IV./JG 3 shot down another nine.

The Eighth Air Force recorded what happened to the 3rd Bombardment Division: "*Immediately after the bombing assault, 30 to 35 Fw 190s and Me 109s began aggressive and vicious frontal attacks with enemy aircraft coming in abreast and flying through formations. At least 15 aircraft were lost in the combination of these attacks.*"

The large number of enemy aircraft destroyed during the day's operations was viewed as a major achievement for the *Staffel*, particularly in the light of the relatively acceptable losses incurred – two Fw 190s. For its part, IV./JG 3, whose new *Kommandeur*, *Hptm.* Heinz Lang took over command from *Major* Friedrich-Karl Müller the same day (who took over as *Kommodore* of JG 3), claimed 25 victories with just one pilot killed and three wounded.

I. *Jagdkorps* reported the loss of 19 aircraft with a further 17 receiving over 60% damage. Thirteen pilots were reported killed, 17 wounded and another 24 missing.

The Eighth Air Force reported 12 B-24s and 33 B-17s lost, including 11 which landed in neutral Sweden as a result of battle damage.

Thursday, 13 April 1944

Once again, aircraft manufacturing facilities were the targets for the Eighth Air Force as the American offensive switched to southern Germany. This time it was to be the turn of the ball-bearing factories at Schweinfurt, the Messerschmitt production plant at Augsburg, the Dornier plant at Oberpfaffenhofen and Lechfeld airfield.

By mid-April 1944, USAAF bombing and strafing attacks on Luftwaffe airfields were a constant threat. Here, a Fw 190 of Sturmstaffel 1, covered by camouflage netting, is pushed by mechanics towards its dispersal at Salzwedel. The Fw 190 A-7 to the right of the picture has all the attributes of a Sturmstaffel fighter at this time; spiral-spinner, fuselage identification band and drop tank (on the ground).

Five hundred and sixty-six of the 626 bombers despatched were effective over their assigned targets, escorted by nearly 900 fighters.

Sturmstaffel 1 and IV./JG 3 took-off following an *Alarmstart* at 12.45 hrs, forming up into a *Geschwader*-based *Gefechtsverband* with the *Stab*, I. and II./JG 3. Towards 14.00 hrs, enemy condensation trails were sighted east of Giessen at 6,500 m (21,320 ft), but the formation was flying with an immensely strong escort of P-51 Mustangs. At 14.00 hrs over Aschaffenburg, the German formation launched a frontal attack against the third wave of bombers.

Ignoring the Mustangs and powering through a formation of some 150 B-17s, the Fw 190s of *Sturmstaffel* 1 shot down five *Viermots* in a matter of seconds.

The Eighth Air Force recorded: *"Of the three Bombardment Divisions, 1st met the heaviest air opposition... Around 14.00, another series of attacks was launched 10 minutes before Schweinfurt and continued for about half an hour. The lead Combat Wing, which sustained the heaviest losses was first attacked at about 13.50 near Klingenberg. Eight B-17s of the high group were shot down in about three minutes... Crews reported usual types of attack..."*

The victorious *Sturmstaffel* pilots were *Lt.* Siegfried Müller (5th victory at 13.55, a *Herausschuss*), *Lt.* Werner Gerth (6th victory at 13.55), *Uffz.* Gerhard Vivroux (4th victory at 13.55), *Uffz.* Heinrich Fink (1st victory at 13.55, a *Herausschuss*) and *Uffz.* Karl-Heinz Schmidt (1st victory at 13.55, a *Herausschuss*). IV./JG 3 reported victories over seven enemy aircraft, four of them *Herausschüsse*. Neither unit suffered casualties, with only three Fw190s of IV./JG 3 being damaged and the *Sturmstaffel's* Fw 190 'White 8' flown by *Lt.* Siegfried Müller damaged in a belly landing near Wertheim-am-Main.

Following a meeting between representatives of Messerschmitt and Focke-Wulf based at the latter firm's Bad Eilsen works on this day, a Messerschmitt engineer wrote of the *Sturmstaffel*: *"This* Staffel *consists of hand-picked personnel, committed to extremely hazardous operations...the success of the* Sturmstaffel *has been considered outstanding."*

Friday, 14 April 1944

No operations were conducted by the Eighth Air Force this day, though *Uffz.* Heinrich Fink of *Sturmstaffel* 1 was reported as killed in action near Ebersbach on the Neckar. Details of this action are not known.

Saturday, 15 April 1944

Bad weather with heavy cloud extending to 24,000 ft (7,200 m) returned to haunt the Eighth Air Force and heavy bomber operations were scrubbed once again. For the fighters of the VIII Fighter Command however, it was to be another day of operations. More than 600 P-38s, P-47s and P-51s mounted strafing missions against *Luftwaffe* airfields in north-west and central Germany. One of the targets was Salzwedel where one Bf 109 G-6 of IV./JG 3 was destroyed on the ground.

Fw 190s of *Sturmstaffel* 1 took off in order to defend their airfield, but one aircraft was shot down, the pilot apparently parachuting to safety.

Despite the risks posed by these large American fighter sweeps, the *General der Jagdflieger, Generalleutnant* Adolf Galland, braved a visit to Salzwedel during which he briefed officers of the *Geschwaderstab* JG 3 and *Stab* IV./JG 3 on his plans for the tactical re-engineering of IV./JG 3. These plans would have far-reaching effects on the composition and operations of this unit as well as upon the future of the *Sturmstaffel*.

As a result of the encouraging successes achieved against the bombers by IV./JG 3, Galland wanted to convert the unit into a fully-fledged *Sturmgruppe*. Furthermore, it was Galland's ambition that every *Geschwader* operating in the defence of the Reich would eventually include its own *Sturmgruppe*. Reaction to this proposal on the part of IV./JG 3's pilots appears to have been mixed and led to considerable debate.

Below *Despite the risk of air attack, Generalleutnant Adolf Galland, the General der Jagdflieger, chose to hold an open-air meeting at Salzwedel on the evening of Saturday, 15 April 1944 during which he outlined his intention to expand the Sturm concept to Gruppe strength. The first move in this direction was to be the creation of IV.(Sturm)/JG 3 to be commanded by Hptm. Wilhelm Moritz. Seen sitting on deckchairs in this photograph are those attending this meeting – Galland (left), Moritz (to Galland's left) and Major Friedrich-Karl Müller. Note Fw 190 'White 11' of Sturmstaffel 1 moving along the taxiway and a Bf 109 G-6 of JG 3 parked by the perimeter fence.*

Above *Generalleutnant Adolf Galland walks across the airfield at Salzwedel accompanied by Major Erwin Bacsila of Sturmstaffel 1 (to Galland's right) and Hptm. Wilhelm Moritz.*

Three officers who would each play a leading role in the development of the Luftwaffe's Sturmgruppen. Left, Leutnant Oskar Romm, who served successively on the Gruppenstab of IV.(Sturm)/JG 3 and as Staffelkapitän of 12. and 15.(Sturm)/JG 3. Romm shot down three B-24s in a single attack on 27 September 1944. Centre, Hptm. Wilhelm Moritz, Kommandeur of IV.(Sturm)/JG 3 and, right, Major Walther Dahl, Kommodore of JG 300

Frantic activity around an Sturmstaffel 1 Fw 190 A-7 at Salzwedel as armourers attend to reloading one of the wing-mounted 20 mm MG 151 cannon. Note the stained spinner and overall dark appearance of the cowling.

Though Galland's reasoning was appreciated, many officers felt that it was unnecessary to sign oaths and documents of obligation, let alone volunteering for tactics which would involve ramming or court-martial, when those already employed were achieving results.

It was also known from discussions with pilots of the *Sturmstaffel* that a signature on a piece of paper was not taken very seriously and that, so far, no pilots had been court-martialled or sent to another unit for not ramming an enemy bomber. Most pilots signed the oath simply to avoid complications.

Accompanying Galland on his visit was *Hptm.* Wilhelm Moritz, whom the *General der Jagdflieger* introduced as the new *Gruppenkommandeur*, replacing *Hptm.* Heinz Lang.

Perhaps the most immediate change for the *Gruppe* was the announced replacement of its Bf 109 G-6s by the Fw 190 A, an aircraft better suited for work as a *Sturmjäger*.

Tuesday, 18 April 1944

The onslaught against the German aircraft industry continued with the Eighth Air Force mounting attacks on a range of targets around Berlin including Oranienburg, Perleberg, Brandenburg and Rathenow.

The tactical partnership of *Sturmstaffel* 1 and IV./JG 3 was ordered in to the air at 13.30 hrs, but bad weather prevented assembly with other defending fighters and it was only these two units together with elements of II./JG 302 which carried out a close-formation attack on some 350 B-17s escorted by 100 fighters. Sixty kilometres (37 mls) west of Berlin, *Sturmstaffel* 1 attacked first with *Gefr.* Wolfgang Kosse claiming one of the Fortresses – his 21st victory at 14.16 hrs – and *Uffz.* Kurt Röhrich another a minute later, representing his 8th victory.

Just under 20 minutes later, at 14.35 hrs, *Ofw.* Gerhard Marburg, destroyed a P-51 Mustang.

The unit suffered the loss of one aircraft, but no pilots.

Closely following the *Sturmstaffel*, IV./JG 3 showed its mettle once again by claiming no fewer than 19 B-17s destroyed, though the actual American losses were 19 B-17s in total for the entire mission including one aircraft which was interned in Sweden. Only one pilot was lost from IV./JG 3. This not insignificant accomplishment was deemed sufficient to gain *Major* Friedrich-Karl Müller a mention in the official *Wehrmacht* bulletin of the day.

Wednesday, 19 April 1944

Sturmstaffel 1 and IV./JG 3 were scrambled from Salzwedel between 09.30 and 09.45 hrs to intercept American heavy bomber formations – 744 aircraft in all – heading for the aircraft plants at Kassel/Waldau, Bettenhausen and Altenbauna and the airfields at Eschwege, Lippstadt, Werl, Paderborn and Gütersloh. This force was protected by nearly 700 fighters.

The strength of the fighter escort on this particular day made it hard for IV./JG 3 to get through to the bombers – only five B-17s from the 1st Bombardment Division were lost in total.

Sturmstaffel 1 was ordered to Berlin to cover the capital but made no contact with the enemy.

The results of the day's operations would have an effect on the *Sturmstaffel*. In addition to the fighter escort, a further 500 USAAF fighters conducted sweeps across north west Europe. During one such sweep, *Oblt.* Otto Wessling, a *Ritterkreuzträger* and *Staffelkapitän* of 11./JG 3 with 83 victories to his credit was killed on the ground after he had made a belly-landing in his burning Bf 109. His successor was nominated as *Lt.* Werner Gerth, the man who had led *Sturmstaffel* 1 in combat on several missions.

The officers, pilots and ground personnel of Sturmstaffel 1 assemble in front of the hangar at Salzwedel on 20 April 1944, the Führer's birthday, to listen to an address by their commander, Major Hans-Günter von Kornatzki and to receive awards.

Major von Kornatzki presents awards to four members of his unit. In the photograph below, von Kornatzki shakes hands with a member of the unit's technical team. To his right is Uffz. Kurt Röhrich, whilst looking on from the row of pilots to the left can be seen (from left) Ofw. Gerhard Marburg, Uffz. Heinz Steffen and Uffz. Willi Maximowitz.

Saturday, 22 April 1944

On 22 April, the Eighth Air Force, flushed with its success against the German aero-industry, despatched 779 B-17s and B-24s escorted by 859 fighters, to "lower priority" targets, most of them to the marshalling yards at Hamm.

That day, *Uffz.* Oscar Boesch, a young Austrian pilot, arrived in the city of Hamm en route to his first operational posting with JG 3. Boesch had recently completed his advanced fighter training with JG 101. As he recalls: "Since I was born on 18 May 1924 in Hoechst, Austria, I was lucky enough to have completed full training as a glider pilot before being accepted into the *Luftwaffe* for pilot training in August 1942."

"To be able to qualify for entry into the Fighter Arm, I had to undergo intensive training. I was first in the *Flugzeugführerschule* A/B 118 at Stettin, then I was transferred to JG 101 in Nancy (France) in July 1943 for advanced training on the Bf 109 F and G-6. I must have correctly done what was needed because my transfer to a unit in the defence of the Reich came as early as February 1944, while I was with the *Ergänzungs Jagdgruppe Süd* at Avignon. In April 1944 while I was heading to my first appointment in JG 3, something happened that really influenced my commitments."

Major Hans-Günter von Kornatzki congratulates Uffz. Helmut Keune after another successful mission. Identifiable in this picture are, from left: Lt. Siegfried Müller, Lt. Werner Gerth, Hptm. Fritz Reinsperger, Lt. Rudolf Metz, Lt. Richard Franz, Flg. Wolfgang Kosse (back to camera), Ofw. Gerhard Marburg, Uffz. Willi Maximowitz, von Kornatzki, Keune and Uffz. Oscar Boesch.

"Stopping over in Hamm, the taste of heavy bombardment gave me a real shock... I was there with three other pilots from my training unit and we had driven up from Avignon in the south of France. It was good to be back in Germany. The bombs came down close to the main station... I had to rush down into a basement along with terrorised women and children... When the first bombs landed, the lights in the cellar went out. They lit candles for light. Children cried. I had never been so frightened in my life. There was total panic... I spent a few hours there, in the dark and dust, listening to the bombs falling above our heads. When we got out, the town was nothing but fire and ruins, a place like Hell. The following night, and the night after, the bombs fell again. I made up my mind. I would volunteer for the *Sturmstaffel* then stationed at Salzwedel..."

Between 18.20 and 18.35 hrs, *Sturmstaffel* 1 and IV./JG 3 took off from Salzwedel and were vectored towards the Köln area where they met the 277 B-24 Liberators of the 2nd Bombardment Division. It took over 20 minutes for IV./JG 3 to bring down four of the Liberators, whilst for *Sturmstaffel* 1, it was to prove a fruitless operation.

Mechanics take a break on the wing of an Fw 190 A-7 of Sturmstaffel 1 at Salzwedel in late April 1944. The aircraft is fitted with a 300 ltr drop tank and has the unit's trademark spiral spinner and black-white-black fuselage band.

Monday, 24 April 1944

The Eighth Air Force once again ventured to attack targets in the south of Germany. Seven hundred and sixteen bombers escorted by 867 fighters hit airfields and aircraft plants at Landsberg, Erding, Oberpfaffenhofen, Friedrichshafen, Gablingen and Leipheim.

Sturmstaffel 1 and IV./JG 3 were in the air at 12.00 hrs. Assembling with the Geschwaderstab and I. and II./JG 3, they headed south. According to Lt. Siegfried Müller, contact was made with some 700 bombers and 300 fighters. It was probably because of the formidable fighter escort, that the Sturmstaffel disengaged without success and flew towards Neuburg-an-der-Donau in order to refuel.

However, just before landing, the unit clashed with Allied fighter-bombers and during the encounter, Uffz. Heinz Steffen was forced to bail out. The rest of the unit managed to land safely at Neuburg which had just been the subject of Allied attack.

Saturday, 29 April 1944

"When at noon on Saturday, the sirens wailed over Berlin and a little later, single groups of US gangster aircraft appeared over the capital to drop their terror bombs aimlessly on a wide-spread residential area of the city, the operation rooms of the German air defences had been working at a high pitch for a long time..."

So wrote a German press reporter following the events of 29 April 1944, when Berlin was to be the target once again. It was to be a day during which the pilots of Sturmstaffel 1 would enjoy their greatest success.

The Eighth Air Force committed 368 B-17s and 210 B-24s for its attack on the German capital, whilst 38 B-17s were to attack various targets of opportunity in the Berlin and Magdeburg areas. Escort for the heavies was to be provided by 814 USAAF fighters.

According to the war diary of I. Jagdkorps: "From 07.25 hours, the German intercept service was able to locate the assembly of 11 combat wings. Commencing at 09.15 hrs, 600 bombers, 400 single-engined and 200 twin-engined fighters took off from the Great Yarmouth area to fly an offensive mission in an easterly direction towards Berlin. They crossed the Zuider Zee, towards Hannover and Soltau and struck at Berlin flying by way of Stendal and Pritzwalk."

To meet the Americans, the Jagdkorps was ready to deploy 275 single- and twin-engined fighters.

At 10.10 hrs, Sturmstaffel 1 and IV./JG 3 took off together from Salzwedel led by Lt. Hans Weik. Once assembled with other Gruppen from the Reichsverteidigung over Magdeburg, at 10.45 hrs, the Gefechtsverband headed towards Braunschweig. Shortly before 11.00 hrs, the German formation sighted the American bombers and Weik turned his aircraft 180 degrees to launch a frontal attack.

Simultaneously, and in conformity with its tactical doctrine, the Sturmstaffel formed up for a rearward attack, trusting in its armour plated cockpits to afford it protection whilst closing in to killing range.

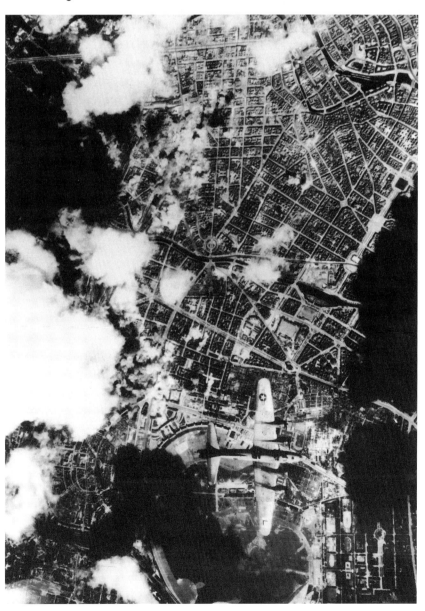

A B-17 flies east over Templehof airport, Berlin, 29 April 1944. To the left, clouds of smoke rise from direct hits to the Templehof marshalling yards and the Anhalter Station. Sturmstaffel 1 accounted for 13 bombers shot down or cut out of formation.

Uffz. Oscar Boesch, seen second from right in this photograph listens attentively to Major Erwin Bacsila as he gives a briefing on tactics. This picture was taken when Sturmstaffel 1 had been dissolved and Bacsila was serving on Gruppenstab of IV.(Sturm)/JG 3. The pilots seen here are members of 11.(Sturm)/JG 3.

One of the more successful pilots in Sturmstaffel 1 was Uffz. Gerhard Vivroux, who scored his fifth victory with the unit on 29 April 1944. Vivroux is seen here whilst with 11.(Sturm)/JG 3. Note the "whites-of-the-eyes" emblem sown onto his jacket, signifying the old pilots' and gunners' maxim "Don't not fire until you see the whites of their eyes". This emblem was warn by many Sturmgruppe pilots and signified the close-range work that they undertook.

Uffz. Oscar Boesch who, as we have seen, had only recently joined the *Staffel* and *Oblt.* Othmar Zehart were two of the successful pilots that day; Boesch remembers: "By the end of April 1944, I arrived early one morning at Salzwedel airfield. I didn't have time to admire the scenery. Instead, I was introduced to my Fw 190 A-7, a 'pure-bred' and massive machine, of which a fellow pilot explained all the refinements before letting me off on a flight as I'd never flown one before! Everything went fine. I made four flights before taking the plane back to the hangar. My initial contact with the aircraft had lasted 60 minutes. My fifth flight took place the following morning, 29 April. It was serious this time; the aircraft was armed and I was sent off against the '*Dicke Autos*'. I didn't have time to be afraid. The *Sturmstaffel* went through the raging defensive fire positioning itself really close from behind to gain optimal efficiency for the attack. In the beginning, attacking the bombers was almost easy. It was exciting. Your adrenalin really pumped. Everybody had their own tactics, your own tricks, but generally we attacked from behind and high for additional speed, offset by 5-10 degrees and about 500 m (1,640 ft) above the formation, opening fire upon the order by radio at 400 m (1,312 ft). The air was pretty thin at 7,200 m (24,000 ft) and often there was a lot of turbulence behind the bomber formation. This sometimes made our approach very difficult. Positioning was also made difficult because of the escort fighters. Zehart, for example, had guts. He flew right into the *Pulk* and we just followed him in."

"When the escort fighters were late to react, we had time to line up – like being on parade, before diving to attack. The bomber gunners usually started to fire and waste their ammunition while we were still out of range at 2,000 m (6,560 ft) from them. It was obvious they were just as scared as we were. Shaken by the slipstream of the B-17s and blinded by condensation trails, we were subjected to machine-gun fire for minutes or seconds that seemed endless before being able to see the results of our attack. Despite the armour plating of our cockpits, we had good reason to dread the defensive fire of the bombers."

"We always went in line abreast. That was our normal tactic. If you went in singly, all the bombers shot at you with their massive defensive firepower, you drew fire from the waist gunners. But as an attack formation, the psychological effect on the bomber gunners was much greater."

"First of all you tried to knock out the tail gunner. Then you went for the intersection between wing and fuselage and you just kept at it, watching your hits flare and flare again. It all happened so quick. You gave it all you had. Sometimes, after the first attack, all your energy seemed to go. Your nerves were burned out. But we had this kind of theory that when you were in the middle of a bomber formation – flying through it – you were, in a way, "protected". The bombers wouldn't open fire because they didn't want to shoot at their own aircraft."

"We would break off the attack just before we were about to collide with our target. The devastating effect of our 30 mm guns was such that we would often fly through a rain of fragments, some being complete sections of aircraft."

By the time the *Sturm* pilots had finished their work, 13 bombers had been shot down or cut out of formation, the best effort so far in the unit's history. *Lt.* Werner Gerth scored his 7th and 8th (*Herausschuss*) victories at 11.07 hrs. One B-17 each was credited to *Fw.* Kurt Röhrich (9th victory at 11.05 hrs), *Uffz.* Helmut Keune (1st victory at 11.05 hrs, (*Herausschuss*), *Uffz.* Gerhard Vivroux (5th victory at 11.05 hrs), *Uffz.* Oscar Boesch (1st victory at 11.07 hrs), *Lt.* Siegfried Müller (6th victory at 11.10 hrs), *Oblt.* Othmar Zehart (3rd victory at 11.10 hrs) as well as another unknown pilot who shot down a B-17 at 11.10 hrs north-east of Helmstedt. *Uffz* Willi Maximowitz added to his score gaining his 4th victory at 11.10 hrs and *Lt.* Richard Franz scored his 4th victory at 11.10 hrs. *Fw.* Wolfgang Kosse scored two *Herausschüsse* (22nd and 23rd victories).

The Eighth Air Force reported: *"The 4A Combat wing experienced difficulty with PFF equipment and lost visual contact with other bombers and fighter escort. Reaching the Magdeburg area, the Wing was attacked by packs estimated as totalling 100 enemy aircraft which attacked in waves from nose to tail. Attacks were pressed home vigourously and closely and lasted for about 20 minutes. The Wing lost a total of 18 B-17s."*

Altogether, the Berlin raid cost the Americans 38 B-17s and 25 B-24s with a total of 18 crewmen killed and 606 missing.

The war diary of I. *Jagdkorps* recorded: *"In spite of good visibility and high numerical strength, the large-scale attack on Berlin was, for the American air force, no success of great importance in respect to the overall war effort. Industry in Berlin sustained only slight damage. Damage to buildings and the losses of personnel were heavy. The strafing attacks on airfields showed no results..."*

The German press were quick to exploit what had been perceived as a failure for the Eighth Air Force and a victory for the *Luftwaffe*: *"One of the biggest air battles ever fought!"* proclaimed a *Luftwaffe* reporter. *"US fighters inferior to Messerschmitts and Focke-Wulfs... The fierce onslaught by German fighters increased in violence when the enemy bombers reached the Berlin area... Any order among the bomber formations was visibly shaken from the moment when the big air battle over the Elbe began..."*

Sturmstaffel 1's losses were four Fw 190 A-7s with 60% damage. *Lt.* Siegfried Müller was forced to belly land in his "White 19" near Jerxheim. *Uffz.* Oscar Boesch also endured an alarming experience as he recalls: *"I had shot down my first bomber, but had to land at Bernburg near Berlin as I was out of fuel. Unfortunately, my landing was on a short airfield, too short for the Fw 190. The Fw 190 flipped over and I was injured and nearly suffocated."*

The month of April 1944, effectively the *Sturmstaffel's* last month of independent operations, cost the unit six pilots and nine aircraft with another six rated at 60% damaged.

More significantly, the day the Americans bombed Berlin, an order was received from OKL redesignating IV./JG 3, under the command of Wilhelm Moritz, to IV.(*Sturm*)/JG 3 in line with Galland's intentions. *Sturmstaffel* 1 was dissolved and its pilots and ground crews formed the nucleus of 11.(*Sturm*)/JG 3 under the command of *Lt.* Werner Gerth.

Led by a cameraman, the pilots of Sturmstaffel 1 make their way past the hangar at Salzwedel towards the dispersal area for a photo shoot.

Left and inset *A candid shot of Sturmstaffel pilots taken moments before or after the photograph below. Major von Kornatzki is standing in the leather coat with his back to the camera.*

Below *Salzwedel, 29 April 1944; one of the last photographs taken of the pilots of Sturmstaffel 1 in front of a Fw 190 before their eventual integration into other units. Seen from left to right, are: Oblt. Othmar Zehart, Lt. Hans-Georg Elser, Lt. Siegfried Müller, Lt. Rudolf Metz, Major Hans-Günter von Kornatzki, Lt. Werner Gerth, Fw. Kurt Röhrich, Lt. Richard Franz, Fw. Wolfgang Kosse, Ofw. Gehard Marburg, Fw. Werner Peinemann, Uffz. Willi Maximowitz, Fw. Josef Groten, Uffz. Oscar Boesch and Uffz. Helmut Keune.*

The pilots of Sturmstaffel 1 walk
briskly across the apron at
Salzwedel, 29 April 1944 having
finished their 'photo shoot'.

Below From left – Ofw. Gehard Marburg, Lt. Werner Gerth,
Fw. Kurt Röhrich and Uffz. Willi Maximowitz.

Sturmstaffel 1 Victories – April 1944

Date	Pilot	Aircraft	Time	Date	Pilot	Aircraft	Time
08/04/44	Uffz. Heinz Steffen	B-24 HSS (3)	14.20	18/04/44	Gefr. Wolfgang Kosse	B-17 (21)	14.16
	Uffz. Kurt Röhrich	B-24 (5)	14.20		Uffz. Kurt Röhrich	B-17 (8)	14.17
	Lt. Siegfried Müller	B-24 (3)	14.20		Ofw. Gerhard Marburg	B-51 (5)	14.35
	Lt. Richard Franz	B-17 (3)		29/04/44	Uffz. Helmut Keune	B-17 HSS (1)	11.05
09/04/44	Fw. Wolfgang Kosse	B-24 (20)			Fw. Kurt Röhrich	B-17 (9)	11.05
11/04/44	Lt. Rudolf Metz	B-24 (2)	11.15		Uffz. Gerhard Vivroux	B-17 (5)	11.05
	Lt. Wemer Gerth	B-24 (4)	11.15		Lt. Werner Gerth	B-17 HSS (7)	11.07
	Ofw. Gerhard Marburg	B-24 (3)	11.15		Uffz. Oscar Boesch	B-17 HSS (1)	11.07
	Uffz. Kurt Röhrich	B-24 HSS (6)	11.15		Lt. Wemer Gerth	B-17 (8)	11.07
	Lt. Siegfried Müller	B-24 (4)	11.15		Lt. Siegfried Müller	B-17 (6)	11.10
	Ofw. Gerhard Marburg	B-24 HSS (4)	11.17		Oblt. Othmar Zehart	B-17 (3)	11.10
	Lt. Werner Gerth	B-24 (5)	11.18		Uffz. Oscar Boesch	B-17 (2)	11.10
	Uffz. Gerhard Vivroux	B-17 (3)	13.18		Uffz. Willi Maximowitz	B-17 (4)	11.10
	Uffz. Kurt Röhrich	P-47 (7)			Lt. Richard Franz	B-17 (4)	11.10
13/04/44	Uffz. Gerhard Vivroux	B-17 (4)	13.55		Fw. Wolfgang Kosse	B-17 HSS (22)	
	Lt. Wemer Gerth	B-17 (6)	13.55		Fw. Wolfgang Kosse	B-17 HSS (23)	
	Uffz. Heinrich Fink	B-17 HSS (1)	13.55				
	Uffz. Karl-Heinz Schmidt	B-17 HSS (1)	13.55				
	Lt. Siegfried Müller	B-l7 HSS (5)	13.55				

Sturmstaffel 1 Losses – April 1944

Date	Pilot	Aircraft	Notes
08/04/44		Fw 190 A-	? % in combat
08/04/44		Fw 190 A-	? % in combat
08/04/44	Lt. Friedrich Dammann	Fw 190 A-7 (340030) White 4	100% in combat NW Kaestdorf, near Fallersleben
08/04/44	Uffz. Walter Kukuk (KIA)	Fw 190 A-7 (643937) White 5	100% in combat 3 km west of Uelzen
08/04/44	Lt. Siegfried Müller	Fw 190 A-7 White 10	? % after combat, Belly landing airfield Salzwedel
08/04/44	Uffz. Karl Rohde (KIA)	Fw 190 A-7 (340340) White 15	100% in combat 6 km west of Fallersleben
09/04/44		Fw 190 A-	? % air attack on Airfield Salzwedel
11/04/44		Fw 190 A-	? % in combat
11/04/44		Fw 190 A-	? % in combat
13/04/44	Lt. Siegfried Müller	Fw 190 A-8 White 8	? % after combat, Bellylanding near Wertheim
14/04/44	Uffz. Heinrich Fink (KIA)	Fw 190 A-7 (431181) White 14	100% in combat 1 km N.E. Ebersbach am Neckar
15/04/44		Fw 190 A-	100% in combat
18/04/44		Fw 190 A-	100% in combat
24/04/44	Uffz. Heinz Steffen (WIA)	Fw 190 A-8 (170091) White 8	100% in combat near Neuburg/Donau
29/04/44		Fw 190 A-	? % in combat
29/04/44		Fw 190 A-	? % in combat
29/04/44	Lt. Siegfried Müller	Fw 190 A White 19-	? % in combat, emergency landing near Jerxheim

EPILOGUE: DISBANDMENT AND EXPANSION

May 1944

During its six month existence, *Sturmstaffel* 1 lost 11 pilots killed and three wounded. Most of its survivors would be killed while serving with subsequent units.

The disbandment of *Sturmstaffel* 1 at the end of April 1944 did not signify the *Luftwaffe's* abandoning of *Major* Hans-Günter von Kornatzki's tactical philosophy. To the contrary, encouraged by the results achieved in such a short time by such a small unit, the OKL decided to establish two new *Sturmgruppen*, II.(*Sturm*)/JG 4 and II.(*Sturm*)/JG 300 in addition to the newly redesignated IV.(*Sturm*)/JG 3.

In mid-May 1944, von Kornatzki received orders to begin setting up and organising II.(*Sturm*)/JG 4 at Salzwedel – though the real formation of the unit would not come about until July of that year. He decided that to assist him in his task, he would need a solid core of pilots from *Sturmstaffel* 1 – pilots who both understood what would be needed of them and who possessed the requisite combat experience. Consequently, *Lt.* Werner Peinemann, *Oblt.* Othmar Zehart, *Fw.* Gerhard Marburg, the still wounded *Lt.* Ulrich Blaese and, eventually, *Lt.* Rudolf Metz (via 11.(*Sturm*)/JG 3), all joined II.(*Sturm*)/JG 4 supplementing an intake of pilots and ground crew drawn from 1./ZG 1, a unit which had previously been employed flying Ju 88s against Allied convoys over the Atlantic and then against Allied invasion forces off Normandy in June 1944. Withdrawn from France and following hasty conversion training onto the Fw 190 at Hohensalza near Posen (Poznan), by the end of July 1944, these pilots constituted the various *Staffeln* of the new *Gruppe*:

Stab II.(*Sturm*)/JG 4	*Obstlt.* Hans-Günter von Kornatzki (newly promoted)
5.(*Sturm*)/JG 4	*Hptm.* Wilhelm Fulda (replaced by *Hptm.* Erich Jugel)
6.(*Sturm*)/JG 4	*Hptm.* Manfred Köpke
7.(*Sturm*)/JG 4	*Oblt.* Othmar Zehart

Fw. Gerhard Marburg flew as von Kornatzki's wingman.

Meanwhile, the recently-appointed commander of IV.(*Sturm*)/JG 3, *Hptm.* Wilhelm Moritz, was working hard to ensure that his *Gruppe's* new role as a *Sturm* unit went ahead smoothly and effectively. Several of his pilots had come from *Sturmstaffel* 1 including Werner Peinemann, Rudolf Metz (who would later go to II.(*Sturm*)/JG 4 with whom he was killed in action), Kurt Röhrich (KIA 19 July 1944), Karl-Heinz Schmidt (MIA 3 August 1944), Gerhard Vivroux (wounded on 12 May 1944 and later died of further wounds on 6 October 1944 suffered whilst with 14./JG 3), Willi Maximowitz (wounded 30 July 1944 and later MIA on 20 April 1945 whilst with 14./JG 3) all of whom went to 11.(*Sturm*)/JG 3.

However, as Moritz recalls: "When I took over the leadership of the *Sturmstaffel* at

On 8 May 1944, Ofw. Gerhard Marburg, above, formerly of Sturmstaffel 1, shot down a B-24 Liberator whilst flying with IV.(Sturm)/JG 3. The sequence below is taken from his gun camera film and shows his approach to his target bomber.

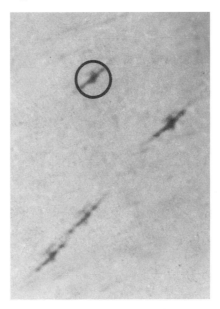

Uffz. Willi Maximowitz of 11.(Sturm)/JG 3 taxies his Fw 190 A-8/R2 'Black 8' at Dreux in France during the Gruppe's operations on the Invasion front in June 1944. The aircraft carries the emblem of JG 3 on its cowling and, in conformity with its type, has 30 mm MK 108 cannon built in to the wings.

Salzwedel, the two ranking officers of the unit, von Kornatzki and Bacsila, were not fit for action; one was ill, the other wounded. I have to admit that my relationship with these two officers was not the best because I had the impression that they allowed their *Staffel* to go into action without their leadership. This was not acceptable practice for responsible officers. In their absence, *Lt.* Gerth led the *Staffel* on operations. For my part, I never accepted the fighting tactic favoured by von Kornatzki and never bound a pilot to ram a bomber. My IV./JG 3 scored many victories attacking bombers with traditional tactics and their successes rested on the sense of duty and the tactics of my men, namely attacking in closed formation and opening fire at close quarters."

An experienced officer blessed with balanced judgement, Wilhelm Moritz was born in Hamburg in 1913. Having briefly commanded 11./JG 1 in Düsseldorf during the summer of 1942, he was subsequently transferred to the Eastern Front where he led 12./JG 51. In the autumn of 1943, he returned to the West and to JG 3.

Some former *Sturmstaffel* pilots were transferred to other units where their experience could best be used. Richard Franz recalls: "At the beginning of July 1944, I arrived at Wunstorf where II./JG 11 was stationed. I had to form up the new 7./JG 11 equipped with the Bf 109. On 12 August, we were ordered to transfer to the Western Front – to Normandy. Throughout the following months, we were engaged in the air and ground battle in France, Benelux and western Germany until February 1945, when we received orders to transfer to the Eastern Front for operations on the Oder river. From then on, it was missions against the Russians – air to air combat and ground attack. On 18 April 1945, my *Gruppe* was relocated to Mecklenburg. I remained in Berlin as the last fighter *Staffelkapitän* in the city. We flew ground attacks inside Berlin which, by then, was surrounded by the Russians. On 25 April, I was shot down by AA fire and fighters."

For those who continued to fly with IV.(*Sturm*)/JG 3 in 1944, there was to be no respite in the battle against the bombers. On 8 May, Berlin and Braunschweig were once again slated as the targets for the Eighth Air Force. Nearly 750 B-17s and B-24s escorted by more than 729 fighters reached Germany, with the B-24s of the 2nd Bombardment Division leading the formation on a straight line to Berlin, passing over the Zuider Zee and onwards, north of Hannover. East of Uelzen, the 2nd Bombardment Division, together with the 45th Combat Wing from the 3rd Bombardment Division which had become separated from the Berlin force, turned south to bomb Braunschweig.

At 08.42 hrs, IV.(*Sturm*)/JG 3 together with the *Geschwaderstab* and the former aircraft and pilots of *Sturmstaffel* 1 were airborne to intercept. At 10.00 hrs, despite worsening weather, contact was made with the B-24s. *Uffz.* Oscar Boesch, a former *Sturmstaffel* pilot, remembers events clearly: "I particularly remember the 8 May mission, the details of which are engraved in my memory and which went wrong from the beginning. We were flying at 3,000 m (9,850 ft) beside a box of B-24s at a slightly lower altitude when our own *Flak* mistook us for a target! A shell exploded near my plane and riddled it with shrapnel. Almost immediately, a trail of oil appeared on my windshield and hood. An oil pipe had been hit. I called on the radio to my comrades that I had to leave the flight. This I did without losing a minute; getting closer and closer to the B-24s. As I flew my plane down through the bomber formation, I found that I had to fire at the last B-24 which burst into fragments. I continued to fire as I flew through the formation but I had no time to observe the results because in a brief matter of time, I had passed through some 60-plus bombers."

"I was in a relatively secure position – in between the bombers where I could not be fired at without the gunners risking hitting one of their own bombers. Out of ammunition and over-excited, I decided to ram one! I moved into an oblique attack on a B-24. I could feel the eddies from the slipstream. My plane was thrown off balance and I missed my intended victim by only a few metres. Then the sky became clear in front of me. Looking around, I could

Uffz. Oscar Boesch of 14.(Sturm)/ JG 3 stands on the wing of his Fw 190 A-8/R2 'Black 14' at Schongau in August 1944.

see no bombers, only some kind of hell of fire. My plane vibrated as shots hit home and I am sure that the lateral armour plating saved my life. Pushing my stick forward, regardless of the terrific negative G forces, I was now in a straight dive, (at 1,000 km/h – 620 mph), - engulfed in bullets and hits. Without wasting time, I undid my harness and ejected the canopy; a freezing wind snatched me from my seat. I felt terrified during my free-fall of 6,000 m (19,685 ft) as I waited to pass through the clouds before opening my parachute. I landed at Goslar in the Harz. I was lucky to have been only lightly wounded in the head by some shrapnel and slightly burned on the face from my fall in the freezing air, because my parachute had been pierced many times by bullets!"

USAAF Intelligence later reported: *"The B-24s attacking Brunswick (sic) were strongly attacked in the target area... Some mass attacks were made, but the majority of passes were made by groups of four to eight, head-on, level, and slightly high out of the sun...The formation was subjected to fierce fighter opposition in the Nienburg area, when nearing Brunswick, without escort. About 75 enemy aircraft, mostly Fw 190s, attacked in a square block formation, massing and assaulting from the nose. These pilots were experienced and viciously aggressive, pressing so closely that in one instance a bomber was destroyed by collision with an enemy fighter..."*

Oscar Boesch was accredited with a B-24 *Herausschuss* following this operation. The other successful pilots of the *Sturmstaffel* this day – all credited with one B-24 destroyed between 10.08 hrs and 10.13 hrs, were *Lt.* Siegfried Müller, his 7th victory, *Uffz.* Willi Maximowitz, his 5th victory and *Uffz.* Karl-Heinz Schmidt, his 3rd victory. However *Oblt.* Othmar Zehart and *Ofw.* Gerhard Marburg each shot down two B-24s, their 4th and 5th and 6th and 7th victories respectively.

Though IV.(*Sturm*)/JG 3's total claims (including those for the former *Sturmstaffel* pilots) amounted to 19 *Abschusse* and *Herausschüsse*, only 11 B-24s were lost in total from the 2nd Bombardment Division and a further seven written off.

On 12 May, the USAAF, using both the Eighth and Fifteenth Air Forces, began its bombing campaign against German oil industry targets, having considered that its prior objective – the neutralisation of the *Luftwaffe* – had been achieved. Nine hundred heavy bombers from the Eighth Air Force, accompanied by a record USAAF and RAF fighter escort, struck oil targets in Germany and Czechoslovakia dropping 1,700 tons of bombs. In the sector controlled by I. *Jagdkorps*, 34 fighters were lost, with another 31 suffering over 60% damage.

Weather hampered further American operations until the 19th, when Berlin and Braunschweig were hit again. On 28 May, a record 1,341 heavies were dispatched against six oil and rail targets in Germany, but nearly 500 were forced to abort due to weather. Against the balance of this force, I. *Jagdkorps* deployed 333 single- and twin-engine fighters of which 266 engaged in combat. I. *Jagdkorps* recorded 39 aircraft destroyed, five missing and 34 badly damaged. The Americans lost 26 B-17s and six B-24s as well as 14 escort fighters.

The next day, the *Korps* readied more than 350 single- and twin-engined fighters to intercept the bombers. In total, 888 of the 993 heavies despatched would attack aircraft industry targets at Cottbus, Kresinski, Posen, Leipzig and Sorau, an oil terminal at Politz and airfields at Rendsburg and Tutow. This force was escorted by a record 1,265 fighters drawn from VIII and IX Fighter Commands.

Towards midday, the 251 B-17s of the 3rd Bombardment Division were nearing Leipzig when the low groups of the 2nd and 4th Combat Wings were attacked by "40 to 60" German fighters making frontal and rear attacks whilst the escort was not present.

B-17G Flying Fortress, (42-31924, coded BG:Q), *Ol' Dog*, was an aircraft of the 344th Bomb Squadron, 95th Bomb Group based at Horham, Suffolk, and was embarking on its 41st mission. Its pilot was 2nd Lt. Norman A. Ulrich; he recalls: "I remember two Fw 190s coming at us, but one in particular seemed to have us in his sights with his

Above *Lt. Siegfried Müller of I V.(Sturm)/JG 3 – and formerly of Sturmstaffel 1 – claimed his seventh victory – a B-24 Liberator – on 8 May 1944. He is seen here in March 1945 as Staffelkapitän of 13.(Sturm)/JG 3. Note the Sturmgruppe "whites-of-the-eyes" emblem sown onto his jacket.*

Below *B-17G Flying Fortress (42-31924, coded BG:Q) Ol' Dog at her crash site near Packebusch on 29 May 1944.*

Inset *Eight members of the crew of B-17G Flying Fortress Ol' Dog photographed in April 1945 whilst they were held as POWs at Mooseburg. Front row, left to right: Ralph Smithberger, George Reiff and Norman Ulrich. Back row, left to right: Rubin Schulman, Norman Phillips, Eugene Buhler, Leon Anderson and Norman Hines.*

Uffz. Karl-Heinz Schmidt of Sturmstaffel 1 and IV.(Sturm)/JG 3 who shot down B-17G Flying Fortress, Ol' Dog from the 95th Bomb Group, one of the 251 aircraft from the USAAF 3rd Bombardment Division which was assigned to attack aircraft plants at Leipzig on 29 May 1944.

Below left *The funeral of Ofw. Gerhard Marburg formerly of Sturmstaffel 1 and II.(Sturm)/JG 4 in Dresden. Marburg was killed in an accident during a routine flight on 3 September 1944.*

Below right *Lt. Werner Peinemann, another veteran of Sturmstaffel 1, takes the salute at the graveside of his comrade, Ofw. Gerhard Marburg.*

cannon blazing away. I could feel the impact of his shells hitting our plane, but at the same time I saw the Fw 190 getting hits and a large piece of it falling off. Suddenly, he began to smoke. Meantime, this Fw 190 had done a good job on us. I remember seeing the Plexiglas nose explode. Cannon shells had made a shambles of our instruments... Our number two engine was hit and windmilling. The radio compartment and bomb bay had been destroyed. Our left gun position had been knocked out... Cannon shells tore off a large chunk of our left rear stabiliser. Air streaming through the nose and the windmilling number two engine caused a severe drag on the plane, which seemed to stop in mid-air."

At around this time, two Fw 190s of IV.(*Sturm*)/JG 3 were returning to Salzwedel from their mission against the bombers. One of these was piloted by *Uffz.* Karl-Heinz Schmidt who had joined *Sturmstaffel* 1 several weeks earlier. As of 8 May, Schmidt had been credited with three victories. Approaching Salzwedel, he spotted the stricken B-17 and manoeuvred to intercept.

Ulrich: "The Fw 190 flew to the right of our cabin and over the wing. You could see him circling to come around for a second attack. I realised it was over at this point, with our only turret knocked out and with wounded aboard. I knew we were about to be shot down in flames so I immediately ordered George (D. Reiff – co-pilot) to lower the landing gear as a sign of surrender."

"While all this was happening, the second Fw 190 was coming in for a side attack. At the last second, he recognised that we were surrendering and wagged his wings, but not before buzzing our cockpit and veering off. He flew so close to our cabin that I thought I could touch him. As we flew on, the two Fw 190s circled us, and you could see them waving in their cockpits and we waved back."

This moment is borne out by one of Schmidt's former *Sturmstaffel* comrades, Oscar Boesch who recalled: "As he (Schmidt) told the story, the B-17 was in bad shape and flew in 500 m above ground level when he intercepted on the flight back to Salzwedel. He flew formation and signalled it to land. After some hesitation, it finally belly-landed into a farmer's field. After landing at Salzwedel, Schmidt drove out to the B-17 to extend 'welcome' greetings. It was still a gentleman's war."

Fw. Karl-Heinz Schmidt was hit by defensive fire whilst attacking a formation of B-24 Liberators on 3 August 1944. He is listed as missing in action.

Obstlt. Hans-Günter von Kornatzki was killed in action on 12 September 1944, in his Fw 190 A-8/R2, W.Nr. 681424 "Green 3". He had been leading II.(Sturm)/JG 4 in action and had shot down a B-17 Flying Fortress at 11.16 hrs, some 30 km (18.5 mls) west of Magdeburg. Pursued by an American escort fighter, von Kornatzki attempted to make an emergency landing but crashed into power lines at Zilly near Halberstadt.

Pilot Roster

BACSILA Erwin, Major. Born 27 January 1910, Budapest, son of an Austrian-Hungarian Brigadier-General. After having studied chemistry at high school in Vienna, he joined the Austrian Army in 1931. Transferring to the Austrian Air Force on 1 September 1935, he was firstly a reconnaissance pilot before becoming a fighter pilot. After the annexation of Austria in 1938, he was appointed Staffelkapitän. During the Polish Campaign (September 1939), he was Gruppenadjutant of II./ZG 1 before being promoted to Staffelkapitän of 11.(N)/LG 2, a night-fighter unit. On 15 September 1940, he took command of 7./JG 52. In November 1940, he was transferred to Romania with a German training unit. In May 1941, he temporarily commanded JG 52 before being assigned to the Stab 3. Jagddivision. He joined Stab/JG 77 in September 1942. He served in Africa until January 1943, before acting as a Jafü in Luftwaffenkommando 3. Served on the staff of Jafü 4 (later Jafü Bretagne) from April 1943 to October 1943. He then joined Sturmstaffel 1 in November 1943 with whom he was wounded in one arm in April 1944 and declared unfit to fly. Posted to Erprobungskommando 16 in May 1944, then to Erg. St. JG 400 in August 1944, I./JG 400 in October 1944 and then as a Staffelführer in JG 301 in November 1944. Appointed Kommandeur of IV./JG 3 in January 1945, before transferring to to Gen. Kdo I. Fliegerkorps. A total of 34 confirmed victories and 8 unconfirmed (one claim with Sturmstaffel 1). Died on 3 March 1982 in Vienna. Last rank: Oberstleutnant. Would have been awarded with the DK i. Gold, though not confirmed.

BIRKIGT Heinz, Uffz. Born 6 September 1920, Insterburg (East Prussia). Birkigt flew with JG 101 in January 1943 before joining 7./JG 26 in October 1943. He volunteered for Sturmstaffel 1 on 7 December 1943. From end of January 1944 with 3./JG 11, where he claimed six victories before being KIA 25 August 1944 when fighting on the Invasion Front. Last rank Feldwebel.

BLAESE Ulrich, Lt. Born 9 June 1924, Berlin. WIA on 30 January 1944. After recovering, probably at the end of 1944, he transferred to 5.(Sturm)/JG 4 where he was KIA on 26 January 1945. Last rank Leutnant.

BOESCH Oskar, Uffz. Born 18 May 1924, Höchst. Boesch was a glider pilot before entering the Jagdwaffe in 1943. Was at A/B Schule 118 in Stettin and then with JG 101 at Nancy in July 1943. Then to the Erg. Gruppe in Avignon in February 1944. Was then posted to JG 3 but volunteered for the Sturmstaffel which he joined a few days before dissolution. 18 claims. Last rank Feldwebel.

DAMMANN Friedrich, Lt. Born 15 Sept. 1921, Bochum. KIA on 8 April 1944. One claim (Herrauschuss). Last rank Leutnant.

DERP Manfred, Uffz-Fhj. Born 24 December 1922, Valparaiso (Chile). With JG 101 in February 1943, before joining JG 26 on 31 October 1943. He left this unit on 7 December to move to Sturmstaffel 1. KIA 30 January 1944. Last rank Uffz-Fhj.

DOST Gerhard, Lt. Born 25 October 1920, Bischoffsburg (East Prussia). KIA 6 March 1944. One claim. Last rank Leutnant.

EHRLICH Günther, Uffz. Born 23 Aug 1923, Duisburg. Ehrlich entered the Luftwaffe in August 1941. Was at the AB Schule Olmutz and Kitzingen, where he qualified for multi-engined aircraft as well as blind-flying. He was later posted to the Jagdwaffe and trained on the Bf 109 and Fw 190 at Stendal and Liegnitz. Volunteered for the Sturmstaffel which he joined on 8 May 1944. Was then with IV./JG 3, with whom he was wounded on 20 August 1944 and 21 March 1945. Last rank Unteroffizier.

ELSER Hans-Georg, Lt. Born 4 February 1923, Eppingen. One of the first members of the Sturmstaffel. MIA in the Ardennes area (St. Vith) on 17 December 1944 whilst with 3./JG 2. Last rank Leutnant.

FINK Heinrich Wilhelm, Uffz. Born 23 February 1922, Goddelau/Darmstadt. KIA 14 April 1944. One claim. Last rank Unteroffizier.

FRANZ Richard, Lt. Born 10 October 1922, Düren. Franz was with JG 27 in June 1942. Served as a flying instructor in EJG Süd in October 1942,

then was transferred to 3./JG 77 in July 1943. He joined Sturmstaffel 1 in February 1944 as one of its earliest members. In July 1944, he was Staffelkapitän of 7./JG 11 until the end of the war. 22 claims. Last rank Leutnant.

GROSSKREUZ Heinz, Uffz. Born 4 November 1921, Hofe, East-Prussia. KIA 1 March 1944 whilst on a ferry flight. Last rank Unteroffizier.

GERTH Werner, Lt. Born 10 May 1923, Pforzheim. Gerth was posted to 7./JG 53 in late summer 1943. Volunteered for Sturmstaffel 1 in January 1944 where he became one of the most successful pilots. Appointed Staffelkapitän of 11./JG 3 on 20 April 1944. Awarded the Ritterkreuz on 29 October 1944 after 37 victories. KIA on 2 November 1944 when Staffelkapitän of 14./JG 3 after having rammed and jumped (his parachute failed to open). Gerth had a total of 27 victories. Awarded with a posthumous Deutsches Kreuz in Gold on 1 January 1945, and was also promoted to Hauptmann after his death.

GROTEN Josef, Fw. Born 30 October 1916 Kleinenbroich. MIA on 3 March 1945 whilst with I./JG 3 but survived the war. Last rank Feldwebel.

KEUNE Helmut, Uffz. Born 10 Feb. 1921, Magdeburg. WIA on 11 May 1944 whilst with 11./JG 3. KIA on 14 January 1945 with 14./JG 3. Six claims. Last rank Unteroffizier.

KAISER, Uffz. Probably transferred early January 1944 to another unit. Fate unknown.

KÖST Walter, Uffz. Born 2 February 1920, Reichenbach. KIA 21 February 1944. Last rank Unteroffizier.

KORNATZKI (von) Hans-Günter, Major. Born 22 June 1906, Liegnitz, Prussia. Kornatzki served in the Reichswehr from 1928. Entered the Luftwaffe in 1933 and was trained as a pilot in 1934 at Schleissheim. In various units (II./JG 132, JG 334, I./JG 136). Kommandeur of II./JG 52 in September 1939. He was then chief instructor at the JFS 1. Then Ia in Stab X. Fliegerkorps, before moving to Stab Höhere Jafü West in February 1943. He founded Sturmstaffel 1 in December 1943 and served as its commander. After the disbanding of the unit, he was appointed Kommandeur of II.(Sturm)/JG 4 but was KIA 12 September 1944. Last rank Oberstleutnant.

Uffz. Kaiser

KOSSE Wolfgang, Flg. Born 27 September 1918, Berlin. Kosse claimed 11 victories with II./JG 26 (the first on 17 May 1940 as a Leutnant). He was Oberleutnant and Staffelkapitän of 5./JG 26 on the Channel Front. Was appointed Staffelkapitän of 1./JG 5 in Norway in 1942 but was banished from his command and demoted to Flieger. Volunteered for the Sturmstaffel where he claimed 6 four-engine kills. Integrated into IV.(Sturm)/JG 3. He regained his rank and took over 13.(Sturm)/JG 3 in October 1944. MIA on 24 December 1944 whilst acting as Staffelführer and Hauptmann with 13./JG 3. A total of 28 claims (the last two on the day of his death).

KUKUK Walter, Uffz. Born 17 July 1921, Klein Altgawischen in East Prussia. KIA 8 April 1944. Last rank Unteroffizier.

LAMBERTUS Erich, Uffz. Born 18 August 1922, Annweiler. He joined 2./JG 26 on 5 December 1943, from 1./EJG Ost. He left I./JG 26 for Sturmstaffel 1 on 10 January 1944. KIA 21 February 1944. Last rank Unteroffizier.

MARBURG Gerhard, Ofw. Born 11 January 1921, Dresden. One of the first members of the Sturmstaffel with whom he was very succesful (5 claims). Was a short time with IV./JG 3 where he made two claims before transferring to Stab II. (Sturm)/JG 4. KIA 3 September 1944 in a flying incident. 7 claims. Last rank Oberfeldwebel.

MAXIMOWITZ Willi, Uffz. Born 29 January 1920, Wuppertal-Barmen. Joined Sturmstaffel 1 early in January 1944. WIA 23 March 1944. WIA again on 30 July 1944 with 11./JG 3. MIA on 20 April 1945 whilst with 14./JG 3. He had 27 victories, 15 of them four-engined (12 B-17s, 3 B-24s). Whilst on the Eastern Front, he shot down 12 aircraft. Was awarded the Deutsches Kreuz in Gold on 1 January 1945. Last rank Feldwebel.

METZ Rudolf, Lt. Born 27 October 1921, Hameln. He entered the Luftwaffe in October 1940 and was trained at JFS 3 and EJG West. In February 1943, he joined 1./JG 5 before being transferred to IV./JG 5. From 23 March 1944, he was with Sturmstaffel 1. On 9 May 1944, he was transferred to 11./JG 3 where he claimed 3 victories on 12 May. On 30 June 1944, he was posted to II. (Sturm)/JG 4 where he attained 5 claims. KIA 6 October 1944 whilst with 6. (Sturm)/JG 4. Awarded the Ehrenpokal on 11 November 1944. 10 claims. Last rank Leutnant.

MÜLLER Siegfried, Lt. Born 13 March 1924, Wilkau. In 1941, Müller was with the LKS Dresden, then with the JFS Zerbst and, lastly, with EJG Süd before joining II./JG 51 in Sardinia in mid-1943. In March 1944, he volunteered for Sturmstaffel 1 and later led 16. and 13.(Sturm)/JG 3 before being posted to JG 7 in April 1945. Total of 17 claims. Last rank Leutnant.

MÜNCH Wilhelm, Lt. Born 23 June 1922, Kocheln. Transferred in March 1944 to Erprobungskommando 25 where he was KIA on 23 March 1944. Last rank Leutnant.

NEUENSTEIN (von) Heinz, Uffz. Born 3 March 1923, Heidelberg. In June 1942, Neuenstein was with JFS 2 and later with EJG Ost. He joined Sturmstaffel 1 at the end of 1943. KIA 30 January 1944. Last rank: Unteroffizier.

PANCHERZ Rudolf, Gefr. Born 19 July 1920, Beuthen. Apparently with Sturmstaffel 1 since the end of 1943 but by February 1944 was with 3./JG 11. He had one claim with JG 11. KIA on 3 March 1944 in a mid-air collision with another pilot from his unit. Last rank Gefreiter.

PEINEMANN Werner, Lt. Born 23 April 1921, Northeim. He enlisted in the Luftwaffe in November 1939 and was in various technical schools until February 1941. Trained in various flying schools, before joining Sturmstaffel 1 on 19 October 1943 from 1./EJG West. WIA 4 March 1944. Posted to 11./JG 3 where he served from 8 May until 21 August 1944. He was transferred to 7. (Sturm)/JG 4 with whom he

was killed on 28 September 1944 in a take-off accident. One claim. Last rank Leutnant.

RÖHRICH Kurt Wilhelm, Fw. Born 21 February 1923, Linz, Austria. With a total of eight claims with Sturmstaffel 1, he was the unit's most successful pilot. Transferred to IV./JG 3 and KIA 19 July 1944 whilst with 11./JG 3. Total of 12 claims. Last rank Feldwebel.

ROHDE Karl, Uffz. Born 19 September 1919, 'Semeritz' near Schwerin (probably Semmritz). KIA 8 April 1944. Last rank Unteroffizier.

SCHMIDT Karl-Heinz, Uffz. Born 20 November 1920, Kiel. Joined the Sturmstaffel in early 1944, with whom he made one claim. After the Sturmstaffel's dissolution, he transferred to IV./JG 3 where he claimed six more aircraft, including a B-24 on 3 August 1944, the day he was reported MIA. Total of seven claims. Last rank Feldwebel.

STEFFEN Heinz, Uffz. Born 13 April 1923, Jünkerath. One of the first members of Sturmstaffel 1 in November 1943. WIA 24 April 1944. Total of 3 claims. Died in the early 1990s.

VIVROUX Gerhard, Gefr. Born 1 February 1923 in Einsiedlerhof near Kaiserslautern. One of the first members of the Sturmstaffel from November 1943 where he made five claims. Transferred to IV./JG 3, with whom he made one claim on 12 May 1944 but was simultaneously wounded. Back at the front, his tally reached 11 claims. Died on 25 October 1944 having been severely WIA on 6 October 1944 whilst with 14./JG 3. Last rank Fw.

WAHLFELD Hermann, Fw. Born 24 December 1920, Hamburg. Early member of the Sturmstaffel. KIA 23 March 1944. Total of three claims. Last rank Feldwebel.

WEISSENBERGER Otto Fw. Born 10 December 1919, Langenselbold. In 1942, he was a pilot with 13. (Z)/JG 5 in Norway, where his brother, Theo, was to become one of the most oustanding aces. Not blessed with his brother's abilities, he volunteered for the Sturmstaffel and received training on the Fw 190. KIA 23 March 1944, probably shortly after his arrival with the unit. Last rank Feldwebel.

ZEHART Othmar, Oblt. Born 17 June 1919, Königswald. One of the first members of the Sturmstaffel from November 1943. He was the first pilot of the unit to register a claim. Transferred for a short time to IV./JG 3 where he claimed two B-24s on 8 May 1944. Joined II. (Sturm)/JG 4 and took over its 7. Staffel. MIA on 27 September 1944. Total of six claims. Last rank Oberleutnant.

Major Hans-Günter von Kornatzki, (centre facing camera), commander of Sturmstaffel 1 and Major Friedrich-Karl Müller, Gruppenkommandeur of IV./JG 3 hold a discussion with the pilots of Sturmstaffel 1 outside the control building at Salzwedel. Recognisable in this picture are (from far left) Gerhard Vivroux, Friedrich-Karl Müller, Heinz Steffen, unknown, Kornatzki, Werner Gerth, Siegfried Müller and Kurt Röhrich.

Selected Source Notes and Bibliography

Interviews and correspondence conducted and written by the authors with former Luftwaffe personnel as listed in the acknowledgements.

Focke-Wulf Flugzeugbau, Bremen – Technischer Außendienst-Truppe, Beanstandungsmeldung Fw 190 Nr.8/44, 24.5.44

Messerschmitt AG, Augsburg – Reisebericht über Reise zu Focke-Wulf am 13.4.44. (18.4.44. Al/Hei.) (via Creek)

PRO/DEFE3/5 Ultra signal of Göring order

PRO/WO208/4170 CSDIC (UK) Report SRGG 128(C) 18 May 1945 (Herget)

Air Staff Post Hostilities Intelligence Requirements on GAF – Tactical Employment Section IV C, HQ USAFE, *Fighter Operations of the German Air Force – Volume 1*, 10 December, 1945 (via Forsyth)

Air Staff Post Hostilities Intelligence Requirements on GAF – Tactical Employment Section IV C, HQ USAFE, *Fighter Operations of the German Air Force – Volume 1*, 10 December, 1945 Appendix XLII *Experiences in Combat against Boeing Fortress II and Consolidated Liberator* – Galland to Operational Units, 1943 (via Forsyth)

PRO/AIR2/7493 *Tactical Notes on the Operations of the Fortresses (B.17F) of the USAAF in the European Theatre of War up to September 15th, 1942*

PRO/AIR40/569 8AF.250 Berlin 6th March 1944

PRO/AIR 40/598 8AF.298 Mission Report and Narrative of Operations, 11.4.1944

PRO/AIR 40/600 8AF.301 Mission Report and Narrative of Operations, 13.4.1944

PRO/AIR 40/613 8AF.327 Mission Report and Narrative of Operations, 29.4.1944

PRO/AIR40/2016 *Heavy Bomber Operations – May 1944* (COPC/S.501/10/INT)

PRO/AIR22/417 AMWIS

PRO/AIR40/639 HQ Eighth Air Force, Intops Summary No. 29

ADI(K) No.373/1945 *The Birth, Life and Death of the German Day Fighter Arm* (via Pegg)

USAFHRC, Maxwell AFB: MACR 5343, 29.5.1944

USAF Historical Studies Nos. 158-160: *The Employment of the German Luftwaffe against the Allies in the West, 1943-1945* by Josef Schmid USAF Historical Division (via Forsyth)

Aders, Gebhard: *Asse aus dem Weltkrieg II – Willi Maximowitz*, Modell-Fan, October 1978

Boesch, Oscar: *"Fortess Hunter"* or *"The Memories of a Focke Wulf 190 Pilot"*, private account by O. Boesch

Caldwell, Donald: *JG 26 – Top Guns of the Luftwaffe* Orion Books, New York, 1991

Caldwell, Donald: *The JG 26 War Diary Volume One 1939-1942* Grub Street, London, 1996

Caldwell, Donald: *The JG 26 War Diary Volume Two 1943-1945* Grub Street, London, 1998

Campbell, Jerry L.: *Focke-Wulf Fw 190 in Action*, Squadron/Signal, Warren, Michigan, 1975

Dahl, Walter: *Rammjäger* Orion Verlag Heusenstamm, Offenbach am Main, 1961

Ethell, Jeffrey and Price, Alfred: *Target Berlin – Mission 250: 6 March 1944*, Janes Publishing Co., London, 1981

Forsyth, Robert: *JV 44 – The Galland Circus*, Classic Publications, Burgess Hill, 1996

Freeman, Roger: *The US Strategic Bomber* Macdonald and Janes, London, 1975

Freeman, Roger A.: *The Mighty Eighth*, MacDonald and Company, London, 1970

Freeman, Roger A.: *The Mighty Eighth War Diary*, Janes Publishing, London, 1981

Freeman, Roger: *The Mighty Eighth War Manual* Janes Publishing, London, 1984

Girbig, Werner, *Jagdgeschwader 5 "Eismeerjäger" – Eine Chronik aus Dokumenten und Berichten 1941-1945*, Motorbuch Verlag, Stuttgart, 1976

Gray, John M.: *Old Dog's Last Flight*, USAF Museum Friends Journal, Vol.16, No.1

Hammel, Eric: *Air War Europa – America's War Against Germany and in Europe and North Africa, 1942-1945* Pacifica Press, Pacifica, 1994

Hoffschmidt, Edward J.: *German Aircraft Guns WW 1-WW 2*, WE Inc, Old Greenwich, 1969

Lächler, Hans: *Sie jagten durch die Bomberpulks*, Jet & Prop 5/95

Middlebrook, Martin: *The Schweinfurt-Regensburg Mission* Penguin Books, Harmondsworth, 1985

Mombeek, Eric: *Defending the Reich - The History of Jagdgeschwader 1 'Oesau'* JAC Publications, Aylsham, 1992

Mombeek, Eric: *Sturmjäger – Zur geschichte des Jagdgeschwaders 4 und der Sturmstaffel 1* ASBL La Porte d'Hoves, Linkebeek, 1997

Obermaier, Ernst: *Die Ritterkreuzträger der Luftwaffe 1939-1945 Band 1 Jagdflieger*, Verlag Dieter Hoffman, Mainz, 1966

Osman, Frank: *Archive - Focke-Wulf Fw 190A*, Container Publications Ltd, undated

Price, Alfred: *Battle over the Reich* Ian Allan, Shepperton, 1973

Prien, Jochen und Rodeike, Peter: *Jagdgeschwader 1 und 11 – Teil 2 1944*, Struve Druck, Eutin, undated

Prien, Jochen: *IV./Jagdgeschwader 3 – Chronik des Einsatzes einer Jagdgruppe 1943-1945*, Struve Druck, Eutin, 1996

Prien, Jochen: *"Pik-As" – Geschichte des Jagdgeschwaders 53 Teil 2*, Struve Druck, Eutin, 1990

Prien, Jochen: *Geschichte des Jagdgeschwaders 77 – Teil 3 1942-1943*, Struve Druck, Eutin, undated

Priller, Josef: *JG 26 – Geschichte Eines Jagdgeschwaders* Motorbuch Verlag, Stuttgart, 1980

Reschke, Willi: *Jagdgeschwader 301/302 "Wilde Sau"*, Motorbuch Verlag, Stuttgart, 1998

Rodeike, Peter: *Focke-Wulf Jagdflugzeug Fw 190 A, Fw 190 'Dora', Ta 152 H*, Struve Druck, Eutin, undated.

Shores, Christopher: *Luftwaffe Fighter Units Europe 1942-45* Osprey Publishing, London, 1985

Swanborough, Gordon & Green, William: *The Focke-Wulf Fw 190* David and Charles, Newton Abbot, 1976

Table of Ranks

The table below lists the wartime Luftwaffe ranks together with their equivalent in the Royal Air Force and the US Army Air Force:

Luftwaffe	Royal Air Force	U.S.A.A.F.
Generalfeldmarschall	Marshal of the RAF	Five Star General
Generaloberst	Air Chief Marshal	Four Star General
General der Flieger	Air Marshal	Lieutenant General
Generalleutnant	Air Vice Marshal	Major General
Generalmajor	Air Commodore	Brigadier General
Oberst	Group Captain	Colonel
Oberstleutnant	Wing Commander	Lieutenant Colonel
Major	Squadron Leader	Major
Hauptmann	Flight Lieutenant	Captain
Oberleutnant	Flying Officer	First Lieutenant
Leutnant	Pilot Officer	Lieutenant
Oberfähnrich	(leading cadet)	(leading cadet)
Fähnrich	(cadet)	(cadet)
Stabsfeldwebel	Warrant Officer	Warrant Officer
Oberfeldwebel	Flight Sergeant	Master Sergeant
Feldwebel	Sergeant	Technical Sergeant
Unterfeldwebel-Unteroffizier	Corporal	Staff Sergeant
Hauptgefreiter		Sergeant
Obergefreiter	Leading Aircraftman	Corporal
Gefreiter	Aircraftman First Class	Private First Class
Flieger	Aircraftman	Private

In addition, the Luftwaffe used the term "Hauptfeldwebel". This was not a rank. A Hauptfeldwebel (colloquially called "Spiess") was the NCO administrative head of a company or corresponding unit (Staffel, battery etc.). His rank could be anything from Unteroffizier to the various Feldwebel.

Glossary

Ergänzungs Jagdgruppe	Operational Training Fighter Group
Experte	'Ace' or skilled pilot
Gefechtsverband	Air battle group
General der Jagdflieger	Commanding General of the Fighter Arm
Generalluftzeugmeister	Chief of aircraft procurement and supply
Gruppe	Group
Gruppenkommandeur	Commander of a Gruppe
Herausschuss	The cutting out of an enemy aircraft from its formation
Jagdgeschwader	Fighter Wing
Jagdwaffe	Fighter Arm
Oberstabsartz	Major in medical service
Pulk	Slang for enemy aircraft formation
Reichsverteidigung	lit. Air Defence of the Reich
Ritterkreuz(träger)	Knights Cross (holder)
Staffel	Squadron
Staffeldienstoffizier	Squadron service officer - administrative
Staffelkapitän	Squadron Commander
Sturmstaffel	Assault Squadron
Viermot	lit. 'Four Motor'. Slang for four-engine bomber

Index